Also by Vince Staten

Ol' Diz
Jack Daniel's Barbecue Cookbook
Unauthorized America
Real Barbecue
Can You Trust a Tomato in January?
Did Monkeys Invent the Monkey Wrench?
Do Pharmacists Sell Farms?

Do
Bald Men
Get Half-Price
Haircuts?

In Search of America's
Great Barbershops

Vince Staten

Simon & Schuster
New York   London   Toronto   Sydney   Singapore

SIMON & SCHUSTER
Rockefeller Center
1230 Avenue of the Americas
New York, NY 10020

Designed by Deirdre C. Amthor

Manufactured in the United States of America

1 3 5 7 9 10 8 6 4 2

Library of Congress Cataloging-in-Publication Data
Staten, Vince, date.
Do bald men get half-price haircuts? : in search of America's
great barbershops / Vince Staten.
p. cm.
1. Barbershops—United States—History. I. Title.

TT957 .S79 2001
646.7'24'0973—dc21   2001020570

ISBN-10: 0-7432-2316-0
ISBN-13: 978-0-7432-2316-4

To Judy—
who's been there through thick and thin,
hair, that is.

Contents

Introduction: "You're Next!"

I'd been putting off getting a haircut for too long. I had that Bozo look—bald men know what I'm talking about; it's our version of a bad hair day. I had braved the elements, shivering down four blocks from my office to a barbershop I had noticed a couple of days earlier. WIB'S, the sign said. I liked the name.

Wib's was crammed into a space between an alley and a donut shop. It was deep, not wide, with a front barely broad enough for a door and a window. My spirits rose as I felt the warm air inside. But as I looked around my mood went in the other direction. Wib was busy chopping on one customer and every seat save one was taken. Before I could turn and fight the wind head-on, a chorus rose from the waiting-room chairs: "You're next!" Seven men were seated around the room, but none of them was there for a haircut. I liked this place already. I've been going to Wib's ever since.

It must have been 1985 or so when the above scene occurred. My longtime barber Lester had died, leaving his shop to his niece, a sharp-tongued woman who wanted all us old customers to know that things were going to be different now. Lester had run too loose a shop. This thing about lolling in the barbershop, reading magazines, idling away the afternoon didn't sit with her. From now on there would be . . . appointments. One by one we slipped away. Some moved down the road to the Holiday Manor Barbershop. Others decided it would be more convenient to get a haircut near their work. Since I worked downtown, I didn't think it would be a problem adopting a new barber and a new shop. I'd done it before.

When my boyhood barber, Roy Lawson, had retired, I shifted two seats down to his son J. Fred. And when I went away to college, I used the campus barbershop. Then hippies landed in America and I didn't even need a barber for, oh, a decade or so. Girlfriends provided a trim when I needed it. It wasn't until I moved to Louisville, Kentucky, in 1978 that I went back to a barbershop. I picked Lester's because it was a half mile from my house, on the way to work, and the price was right: four dollars when I started, if I remember correctly. Then Lester got sick.

Barbershops are personal. Men don't just change barbers at the drop of a hat, so to speak. If the barber doesn't die or we don't move, we'll stick it out, through thick and thin hair. Right now mine is thin, very thin. But Lester's niece had forced me to move. And I moved to Wib's.

Wib Scarboro's Barbershop on Fifth Street in downtown Louisville is a four-chair shop, room enough for four barbers. But it's down to one barber now: Wib. The other three chairs remain, a reminder of flusher times. On this Thursday in September regulars are perched in the two empty barber chairs. The waiting room is full, too, except for one solitary chair in the rear. A visitor would be tempted to turn around and head elsewhere rather than fight the wait.

Wib's Barbershop may be full, but no one's there for a haircut. They've come for the company, and it is available in abundance this afternoon. "Open the door to this barbershop and the lies just pour out onto the street," says Don Miller, a longtime customer. "This is the place for decent haircuts and great stories," he jokes. And the crowd whoops. "Wib doesn't give a haircut worth a damn but the conversation is wonderful," he adds.

Wib Scarboro is not one to take a punch without fighting back. "Don, I've seen better heads on cabbage. . . . In fact, I've seen better heads on a ten-cent beer." And the group whoops some more.

Barbers have been around at least since the days of Samson. In fact the regulars at Wib's might say he's been around that long, too. Not quite. Wib Scarboro's shop has been in existence since 1880, in the same location since 1935. He's been cutting hair since the beginning of Ike's second term,

1956. That's a lot of years circling that chair. At first Wib worked for Clyde Hodges. "He was an old song-and-dance man. I worked for him for ten years, bought the place in '66, and he worked for me for ten years!"

Ben Bodie, an industrial fan salesman from South Carolina, is in the chair at Wib's. He has been directed to the place from the Delta Lounge, a tavern around the corner. Bodie is on a lifelong quest to find America's best haircut. "Last month I got one in Detroit. Before that San Francisco." And how does Wib compare? "This young man's got a steady hand and he knows what he's doing." The gang suggests Wib's steady hand is the product of a refreshing beverage. Bodie appreciates the humor but he wants everybody to know that Wib knows his stuff. "I guess the next time I need a haircut I'm gonna have to figure out a route back through Louisville."

School is letting out and young boys are lining up along the walls in the barbershops around town. Except at Wib Scarboro's. Wib is putting his clippers back in the drawer. He says he has the best hours of any barber cutting hair: "Monday through Friday eight to two, or whenever I get tired. Or someone wants to go fishing. Or squirrel hunting."

I've visited some great barbershops over the past two years while researching this book: Three Brothers Barbershop in Stamford, Connecticut; Vernon Winfrey's Bar-

bershop in Nashville, Tennessee; Hugh Sample's Barbershop in Boomer, West Virginia. I've been in more than
three hundred total. I couldn't get that many haircuts in a
year, of course, so sometimes I'd get a shave. Sometimes
I'd just sit and visit. They allow that.

Floyd's City Barbershop in Mount Airy, North Carolina, is like every other barbershop—the row of chairs,
the facing mirrors, the line of barbers in white smocks.
The whir of electric clippers competes with the chattering on the AM radio, except that they seem to comple-
ment each other. The Polaroids on the wall, the
shoeshine stand in the back, the music on the radio.
Every barbershop is alike. And yet each is unique. In one
the radio may be blaring stock-car racing, in another
Rush Limbaugh. The smell of one leans toward lilac; another smells more woodsy. But what really sets apart each
barbershop is the swirl of people. Some barbershops attract the politicos and conversation steers toward cam-
paigns and electioneering. Another draws the NASCAR
crowd: the radio is a jumble of screaming announcers and
buzzing high-performance motors. Here the talk is baseball; there it's hunting. But it's always interesting. It's life
in the neighborhood.

What makes for a great barbershop? To begin with, it
can't be called a style shop. In fact, if it's called a style
shop, I won't go in. I don't want a hairstyle. I want a haircut. But it goes beyond that. If it's called a style shop, it's
trying to be something other than a barbershop. And I
don't want that. I want a barbershop, a community of

men, where smoking is still accepted, even applauded, even though I don't smoke. Where the radio plays loudly with the sounds of a sports announcer. And where the currency is talk. You learn more in the barbershop than you ever learn in the newspaper. The barbershop is the community center in many places. That community may be an entire small town or a neighborhood. Or it may just be a community of like-minded folks. Give me an old-fashioned barbershop any day (except Sundays and Mondays, of course. All barbershops are closed Sundays and Mondays). The barbershop of my childhood differed not one iota from Wib's. Some things never change.

You can tell a lot from the name. A great barbershop has somebody's name on it. Wib's Barbershop just sounds like a great place to get a haircut. Wib presides over a daily gathering of lawyers and politicos in his shop across the street from the courthouse. The place is full of men just hanging out, debating the latest courthouse scandal and discussing the new server down at the Delta Lounge. That's a barbershop. And the good news is there are thousands of them still out there. Supercuts, Fantastic Sam's, and the chain shops haven't put all the old barbers out of business. Not like hippie hairstyles did back in the sixties and seventies. As eighty-eight-year-old West Virginia barber Hugh Samples told me when I eased into his chair, "Hair's always gonna grow. And somebody's gonna have to cut it. Might as well be me."

When I began this book, I thought I was doing a book about barbershops. What I soon discovered was that I was really doing a book about barbers. Barbers make the barbershops. Like barbecue joints they don't do well as franchises. Folks want idiosyncrasy in a barbershop and a barbecue joint. So no two barbershops are alike because no two barbers are alike.

Oh, and I have learned a ton. My barber, Wib Scarboro, taught me how a barbershop works. San Jose barber Frank Chirco taught me the history of barbering. And Ohio barber Ed Jeffers taught me a lot of new barber jokes.

Everything I've learned, every story I've heard, every joke I've laughed at in my research has lead me back to one thing: my own barber history.

Ask ten men to name the barber who gave them their first haircut. Then ask the same ten men to name their childhood doctor. I'll bet you more can name the barber than the doctor. Roy Lawson gave me my first haircut—sat me up on a little board balanced on the chair arms. I don't remember that very first haircut; I was much too young. But because I was the firstborn, the occasion was duly recorded by my mother in my baby book, *Our Baby— The First Five Years,* a Whitman Publishing scrapbook with a pink and blue cover adorned with a drawing of the ugliest baby you have ever seen.

My first haircut, as recorded on page nineteen, was on August 5, 1948, my first birthday. My mother wrote, "He was a very good boy while having his hair cut. Laughed part of the time and looked at a magazine."

On the first haircut page are before and after photos along with a lock of my hair: a dirty blond color that I haven't seen on my head since. In the before photo my hair is parted at the left crest and combed straight over in the style of the day. In the after photo my hair is sheared close on the sides and piled up on top in a style I also haven't seen since. It looks like a jelly roll and I'm sure my mother cried all night about it.

That first haircut was at Sword's Barbershop, a half block from my house. Most neighborhoods had a neighborhood barbershop in the forties and mine was no different. Sword was Al Sword, a stubby bald man who was never without his white smock shirt. But I got my first haircut from the man at the second chair, a swarthy fellow, thick of build but not fat. His name was Roy Lawson, and if I were to show you a picture of him, you would look at his thick shock of coal black hair, lacquered and sculpted, and say, "He's a preacher, isn't he?" And you'd be right. Roy Lawson was a Free Will Baptist preacher. He cut hair at Sword's Tuesday through Saturday and preached on Sunday. For the first couple of hundred haircuts—I went every other week in the fifties; everybody did—my father would lift me up onto a board that Mr. Lawson positioned across the arms of his barber chair. That put my head at his chin level and made it easier for him to get my sideburns straight. By the time I started going to the barbershop electric clippers were the norm. I never saw a barber use hand clippers then, although I have seen them since. My barber, Wib Scarboro, says his daddy used to cut his hair with hand shears. "He had to squeeze them to cut. They never were sharp enough and I tell you I think he pulled as much of my hair out as he cut."

Sword's was a stock-car barbershop, which meant that no matter what was happening in the outside world—Ike was raising taxes, Governor Clement was speaking at the Democratic convention—the talk at Sword's was about stock-car racing. I grew up in east Tennessee, just a skip over the mountain from the moonshine country of western North Carolina immortalized in the Robert Mitchum movie *Thunder Road*. Dirt tracks were everywhere. Men in New York may have idolized DiMaggio, but men in east Tennessee idolized Junior Johnson and Fireball Roberts, two of the top drivers on the nascent NASCAR circuit. Johnson was from the Asheville, North Carolina, area and became a stock-car driver after a successful career running moonshine and outrunning highway patrolmen. He was the hero at Sword's. I can remember on occasion a stranger would wander in, hear the buzz of stock-car racing on the portable radio, and announce his partiality to Fireball Roberts. The hum of the clippers would come to a stop while one or another of Sword's minions spoke his peace on Junior Johnson's side.

If you were to blindfold me today, spin me around five times, and lead me into Sword's Barbershop, I could tell you exactly where we were; I wouldn't need a single visual clue. I could even tell you with earplugs in. Sword's smelled like Sword's. And it was the most inviting smell of my childhood short of the candy counter at JCPenney. I don't think you could recreate that smell today—you couldn't find the ingredients. Who sells hair tonic? The first aroma when you hit the door was light and fresh but not flowery—the powder, my barber Wib speculates. Then a pungent floral smell would enter your nose. Maybe Lucky Tiger, says Wib, the most popular hair tonic of the fifties. There was also a woodsy note. After asking what a woodsy note is, Wib indicates there are lots of woodsy notes in witch hazel. By the time you reached your chair, there was also a bit of an electric smell mixed in. Somebody had a short in their clippers, says Wib.

Finally, as a young haircut customer, the big day came, and a proud day it was. "That was the day you grew up," says Bruce Haney, a friend since grade school. What transpired was that the barber finally said, "Aaa, you don't need that board no more," and sat you down on the lush upholstered seat of the barber chair. It was only then that you realized that the board was a board—hard and uncomfortable. The seat—now that was a seat, inviting and surrounding. Going to school is a big step in any kid's life. But moving from the board to the seat in the barbershop—that's the first rite of passage.

Mr. Sword retired sometime in the late fifties and the guy who bought his store turned it into a shoe repair shop. Mr. Lawson and the remaining barbers migrated across the street into a storefront in the corner slot of Brickey's Motel.

I liked the move. I got to keep my regular barber and I

no longer had to cross the street. The new shop was just three doors down from my house, a thirty-second bike ride. Mr. Lawson took the first chair—meaning it would be Lawson's Barbershop—with Virgil Crawford at the center chair and J. Fred Lawson, Roy Lawson's beefy, baldheaded son, at the back chair.

Mr. Lawson brought innovation to our neighborhood barbershop, installing a TV so that if he tilted your head just right, you could watch the ball game on Saturday afternoon while he buzzed off your hair.

The first big shock of my early adolescence came when I was twelve and Mr. Lawson announced to me one Saturday afternoon that he was retiring. He was the only barber I had ever had. He knew my cowlick like it was his own. He knew just where to clip my front lock so that it wouldn't curl like a sissy's. He was turning me over to J. Fred, he said. I still remember my thought: J. Fred is bald.

I had watched J. Fred out of the corner of my eye for several years and I wasn't sure I was ready to move two seats down. But I didn't have a choice. I couldn't bear the thought of changing barbershops, too. I would move two seats down.

Hello, J. Fred.

It turned out I liked J. Fred. He was nothing like his dad, and it wasn't just the lack of hair. No, J. Fred cussed. Mr. Lawson was a preacher, a friendly, easygoing Baptist preacher. Profanity never crossed his lips. If his razor slipped and nicked his finger, it was, "My land!" If J. Fred pinched his finger in the dusting powder drawer, it was a string of expletives that began with #!$#! and ended with a whole lot worse. J. Fred liked baseball, not stock-car racing; Pepsi instead of RC; and dirty jokes better than anything. And he cut my hair just like his father had, with a firm but gentle touch.

I hadn't been with J. Fred more than a couple of months when he asked me one day, "Have you thought about a new haircut?" No, I hadn't. I had worn my hair in an early Elvis cut since I was one year old. My hair was "short on the sides, medium on top and leave the sideburns."

"Lots of the boys are wearing these flat tops," J. Fred said. I was preparing to enter junior high and I was starting to notice girls; I was ready. "Go for it," I said. Or the 1959 equivalent.

My mother cried that night. Something about her baby.

My barbershop adventure had begun. And so begins ours. . . .

The reason I went to my barbershop wasn't because J. Fred gave such good haircuts—it isn't rocket science— but because I was comfortable there. So when I set out early in 1999 researching this book, I wasn't looking for the guy who had won the National Haircutting Championship (not that there is one). I was looking for a place where I could sit down in the waiting area, listen to some great conversation, maybe even learn a little about the local community.

I tried for the old geographic spread. I got a shave from Big Bob in Fort Lauderdale. I chatted up the gang at Three Barbers in Stamford, Connecticut. I got a haircut in the far northeast corner of Tennessee at Claude Russell's and in the far southwest corner at Jim's in downtown Memphis.

I talked barbering with Jimmy Knauss, head of the California Barber Board, and Ken Shaddy, a Hall of Fame barber who got his start in the Big Sky country of Idaho.

Floyd gave me a haircut in Georgia, North Carolina, and West Virginia.

I got a trim from a guy who started cutting hair when Herbert Hoover was president. And I learned about haircut competitions from a kid who was born shortly after Reagan was elected.

I even visited the Barbershop Museum and Barber Hall of Fame in Ohio.

I now know everything about barbering except how to cut hair. And I didn't want to learn that anyway. If I did, I would have gone to barber college.

What I did discover is that barbers are the same all over. Sure, Martino at Three Barbers in Connecticut is a little imperfect with his English, despite the fact that he came over from Italy three decades ago. But that doesn't keep him from participating in the insult-fests that go on all day long in his barbershop. When I asked Nick, the lead barber at Three Barbers, if Martino was his brother, he replied, "No, he's my grandfather." Martino immediately let out with a wail. "His grandfather! I'm-a his nephew."

In visiting three hundred and some barbershops, I never felt unwelcome or uncomfortable. A few were a bit sterile, and by that I mean that they were devoid of personality; but there are people who don't want lively conversation with their haircut. Some men don't want to be bothered—just shave and shut up.

Not all barbers are extroverts either. There are—and this may be hard to believe—quiet barbers.

I found it all in my odyssey. In one shop all the spare chairs were occupied by vagrants from the neighborhood. In another the spare chair was filled by a giant furry sleeping cat.

In one neighborhood shop a young boy helped me off with my coat and hung it up. In another a kid dusted me off when I was finished.

Some barbers asked if I wanted my eyebrows clipped. Others did it without asking. A few barbers shaved my neck with a straight razor and shaving cream; most trimmed with an electric clipper. Two barbers even clipped my nose hairs.

I wasn't always entertained or enlightened but there wasn't a single shop that I didn't leave feeling fresher than when I went in. And I smelled that way, too, thanks to an assortment of bottled potions and bracers.

So hop in the car with me, slick back your hair, and let's head out on a barbershop odyssey.

And don't forget to pack your comb.

Chapter 1

A Bunch of Guys Named Floyd

Every time I begin a book I look up my old friend Tom Jester. I learn more eating dinner with him than I learn watching a season of *Who Wants to Be a Millionaire*. He grew up in Fort Payne, Alabama, a place where smart boys get a lot of time to think.

Tom is now the advertising genius of Knoxville, Tennessee—two hours down the road from my hometown—so I met him at a local Mexican restaurant hoping for some wisdom.

"Barbershops, huh? You wrote that book about hardware stores [*Did Monkeys Invent the Monkey Wrench?*]. You know the difference between hardware stores and barbershops, don't you?"

With Tom, you don't interrupt. Once he gets on a roll, you just get out of the way.

"The name. If you wandered into a strange town and saw Wilborn's Hardware right down the street from Wilborn's Barbershop, you'd probably think the store owners were brothers. And you'd be wrong. Unless the barber is named Wilborn Wilborn."

It was an epiphany to me and it was right. Barbershop names don't work like hardware store names.

"The hardware store would be owned by someone with a name like Roy Wilborn. The barbershop, on the other hand, would be owned by someone with a name like Wilborn Carrico. That's the way it is in naming stores: barbershops use the owner's first name; hardware stores use the owner's last name."

Tom even had a theory about the root cause.

"Barbers want you to know it's a friendly place, where folks call each other by their first name. Hardware guys want you to know it's a professional operation—those braces you're buying will in fact hold up a roof."

It would be a year before I would fully appreciate Tom's theory but he was right. In my travels for this book I found only a handful of barbershops that use the owner's last name. And that's why the number one, most popular name for a barbershop is Bob's—Bob's Barbershop—followed by John's Barbershop, Jim's Barbershop, Tom's Barbershop, and Floyd's Barbershop. The reason for the last one is obvious to anyone who owns a television set. The genial barber just down Mayberry's Main Street from Sheriff Andy Taylor's office on *The Andy Griffith Show* was Floyd the barber.

I've been in five of those twenty-three Floyd's Barbershops and only one of them was actually owned by a guy named Floyd: Ed Floyd has a barbershop in Buford, Georgia, just north of Atlanta. When your last name is the same as the first name of America's most famous barber, it's pretty clear what to do.

The most famous Floyd's Barbershop is in Mount Airy, North Carolina, Andy Griffith's hometown and a model for TV's Mayberry. Floyd's City Barbershop at 129 North Main Street is owned by Russell Hiatt, who's been cutting hair in Mount Airy since 1948, when Andy Griffith was in high school there. Andy frequented Russell's shop back in the days when it was known simply as City Barbershop.

Over the years barbers have come and gone at Hiatt's place, a hundred or so he estimates. "And not a one of them was ever named Floyd." He says *The Andy Griffith Show* people made up the name of Floyd's Barbershop. But Hiatt says they didn't make up the character, not completely anyway. Russell is Floyd. "Of the barbers we've had in here, I look the most like Floyd. And I talk the most like him."

Floyd's isn't a cute name; it's an apt name. One thing I love about barbershops is they don't get cute with their names, like beauty shops do. There's no Curl Up and Dye Barber Shop like there is a beauty salon in Kingsport, Tennessee. Just down the road from my son's school in Crestwood, Kentucky, is a beauty salon called The Hair Port, no place I'd want to get a haircut. Beauty salons have names like that: A Cut Above (Mayfield, Kentucky), Hair Affair (Twin Falls, Idaho), and Karen For Hair (Monaca, Pennsylvania).

Barbershops have names like Virgil's (Phenix City, Alabama), Herman's (Lodi, California), and Elmo's (Ketchikan, Alaska).

A look at barber names is like a trip down memory name lane. Barbers seem to have the kinds of names that fell out of favor about the time the Hindenburg fell out of the sky—old-fashioned names like Chester, Ernest, Virgil, Elmo, Cecil, Kermit, Abner, Herman, Milt, Lamar, Wilbert, Thurman, Garland, Alvin.

In fact the barbershop may be the last stronghold for fellows with names like Virgil and Herman and Elmo . . . and Earl and Claude and Roy.

But I'm getting ahead of myself. Before we begin our barbershop odyssey, we need to backtrack to the origins of this book, and farther, to the origins of the haircut.

Chapter 2

From Hair to Eternity

Before we can begin our barbershop adventure perhaps we should sit back (in a barber chair) and ask ourselves how it is we got to the point in human evolution where we have a need for barbers.

Whither barbers?

And whither hair?

Hair, simply put, is protein.

Steak is protein.

Beans are protein. So why aren't beans growing out of your scalp or steaks hanging from your head?

Actually it's because hair is a different kind of protein, a hard fibrous type known a *keratin*. And hair is dead protein. It doesn't grow so much as it is pushed up from the living cells in the scalp. It continues to increase in length until you see a barber or find it in the shower drain, which could be between two and six years after it begins its journey out of your scalp, depending on the gene code you inherited from crazy grandpa Harry. That's the life expectancy of a hair follicle: two to six years. Hair grows, on average, half an inch a month—six inches a year.

So hair is dead protein. And it's a good thing it's dead; otherwise think how painful it would be to get a haircut. Barbers would be less popular than dentists and everyone would be as shaggy as those ZZ Top fellows.

In the beginning we were all hairy. Hairy from the tops of our sloped little heads to the bottoms of our padded little feet. We weren't exactly human yet; we were still in that evolutionary phase we used to call the missing link. But we were on the way to hominid form. And somewhere along that highway we lost our fur.

How that happened, we still aren't sure.

Humans have always had hair although that may not be true in the future.

Hair remained a characteristic of *Homo sapiens*. The first humans to walk the earth, or walk upright on the earth, were hairy fellows, hardly distinguishable in coat from the ground sloths and wooly mammoths that roamed the plains, snacking on these hairy men.

Hair has steadily retreated: it is now concentrated on the head, under the arms, and in the crotch area. Except for those repulsive guys at the beach with a blanket of fur on their backs, most of the rest of the body's hair is sparse and downy in texture. Evolutionary scientists predict that in the future, most of that hair will disappear, but to an evolutionary scientist, the future is measured in millennia. We will have hair as long as this book is in print.

Hair has evolved to the point today that too much or too little of it will cause psychological and social pain. But in prehistoric times hair had no cultural function. It was all biology. It provided insulation, holding in heat during the cold winters of the Ice Age and keeping out the warmth of the Jurassic sun. It acted as a sensory organ (think of the whiskers of a cat and the quills of a porcupine). It helped cool the body through the release of perspiration and rid the body of unwanted hormones from the glands. There were even immune cells at the opening of the hair follicle that detected germs and the like on the skin's surface and powered up the immune system.

One hair is about .03 of a millimeter thick. Hair is thin but it's as strong as a wire of iron. It takes a force of about 130 pounds before a hair will break.

Your hair begins to grow even before you are born—not that this is a great revelation to anyone who has ever been present in the delivery room. Babies are born hairy. This baby hair begins to grow around the third month after conception. The hairs start out as what biologists call trichocysts, then develop into hair follicles as the fetus grows. They eventually become the familiar downy hair that covers the newborn.

The number of hairs you are born with is the number
of hairs you will have—period. It never increases. Maybe
instead of immediately running to count fingers and toes,
nervous parents should instead count hair follicles. After
all, you can cover up a six-toed baby with those cute itty-
bitty Nikes. But a hairy baby girl will grow up to be a
hairy woman, only able to secure dates through Internet
Hairy Women sites.

The number of hairs on the head varies from person to
person and can range from a mere 60,000 to as many as
150,000. That number is usually connected to your hair
color. Blond hairs are thinner than brunette hairs so
blondes tend to have more of them while brunettes have
fewer.

Why am I a brunette and you a blonde? It goes back to
grandpa Harry and his gene pool. Hair color comes from
the pigment cells sent to the hair. The more pigment the
root sends to the hair, the darker the hair becomes. And
what determines the amount of pigment sent is a genetic
secret, although in the last half century Clairol may have
had more to say about hair color than has genetics.

But the head isn't the only hairy place. On average humans have about 1.4 million hairs on their body, only
about 450,000 of them on the head and neck. (The beard
and mustache are comprised of about thirty thousand
hairs.)

Frankly there's hair everywhere.

The only place we don't have it is on the palms of the
hands and the soles of the feet. (If you have hairy palms,

you must not have taken to heart your mother's warnings about self-pleasure. And if you have hairy soles, you should contact P. T. Barnum, c/o Ringling Bros. And Barnum & Bailey.)

Hairs on different parts of the body grow at different rates. Beard hair grows fastest, a little over half an inch a month. The hair on the top of the head is next with a rate right at half an inch a month. Armpit hair grows a little less than half an inch a month. The slow growers are the eyebrows and pubic hair at about a quarter of an inch a month. So why don't you have a beard hanging under each arm and sideshow eyebrows? Because those hairs have shorter life expectancies (two to three months for an eyebrow hair). They fall out before they get embarrassingly long.

We don't know how fast ear hair grows; no one has studied it. No one wants to.

The season also affects hair growth. Hair grows faster in spring and summer than in fall and winter.

We are a hairy people, but not nearly as hairy as our ancestors. And I am not talking about grandpa Harry here but those early humans who wandered the Serengeti thousands of years ago. Why were they so hairy and why are we so denuded of hair?

Why we lost our hairiness was a question that vexed even the father of evolution, Charles Darwin. Writing in

The Descent of Man, and Selection in Relation to Sex, he was not sure our dearth of hair—compared to, say, a grizzly bear—was an advantage. "The loss of hair is an inconvenience and probably an injury to man, even in a hot climate, for he is thus exposed to the scorching of the sun, and to sudden chills, especially during wet weather. As Mr. [Alfred Russel] Wallace remarks, the natives in all countries are glad to protect their naked backs and shoulders with some slight covering. No one supposes that the nakedness of the skin is any direct advantage to man."

So why are we naked, or nude of hair, compared to bears and two-toed sloths?

Darwin chewed on the hair question for many pages.

"Another most conspicuous difference between man and the lower animals is the nakedness of his skin. Whales and porpoises, dugongs and the hippopotamus are naked; and this may be advantageous to them for gliding through the water; nor would it be injurious to them from the loss of warmth, as the species, which inhabit the colder regions, are protected by a thick layer of blubber, serving the same purpose as the fur of seals and otters. Elephants and rhinoceroses are almost hairless; and as certain extinct species, which formerly lived under an arctic climate, were covered with long wool or hair, it would almost appear as if the existing species of both genera had lost their hairy covering from exposure to heat. This appears the more probable, as the elephants in India which live on elevated and cool districts are more hairy than those on the lowlands.

"May we then infer that man became divested of hair from having aboriginally inhabited some tropical land? That the hair is chiefly retained in the male sex on the chest and face, and in both sexes at the junction of all four limbs with the trunk, favors this inference—on the assumption that the hair was lost before man became erect; for the parts which now retain most hair would then have been most protected from the heat of the sun."

But then Darwin bolts upright. What about the head, what about the head?

"The crown of the head, however, offers a curious exception, for at all times it must have been one of the most exposed parts, yet it is thickly clothed with hair. The fact, however, that the other members of the order of primates, to which man belongs, although inhabiting various hot regions, are well clothed with hair, generally thickest on the upper surface, is opposed to the supposition that man became naked through the action of the sun. Mr. [Charles] Bell believes that within the tropics it is an advantage to man to be destitute of hair, as he is thus enabled to free himself of the multitude of ticks and other parasites, with which he is often infested, and which sometimes cause ulceration. But whether this evil is of sufficient magnitude to have led to the denudation of his body through natural selection, may be doubted, since none of the many quadrupeds inhabiting the tropics have, as far as I know, acquired any specialized means of relief."

This led Darwin to one conclusion—and an important one for him: "His body therefore cannot have been divested of hair through natural selection. Nor, as shown in a former chapter, have we any evidence that this can be due to the direct action of climate, or that it is the result of correlated development."

We didn't lose our hairiness naturally, he says. "The view which seems to me the most probable is that man, or rather primarily woman, became divested of hair for ornamental purposes, as we shall see under Sexual Selection."

He uses the example of the monkey to illustrate sexual selection of hairlessness. "We know that the faces of several species of monkeys, and large surfaces at the posterior end of the body of other species, have been denuded of hair; and this we may safely attribute to sexual selection, for these surfaces are not only vividly colored, but sometimes, as with the male mandrill and female rhesus, much more vividly in the one sex than in the other, especially during the breeding-season. . . . The hair, however, appears to have been removed, not for the sake of nudity, but that the color of the skin may be more fully displayed. So again with many birds, it appears as if the head and neck had been divested of feathers through sexual selection, to exhibit the brightly-colored skin."

So we lost our hairiness because we wanted to look better and prettier. We willed away our coat.

On this one Darwin is pretty much in the barber chair alone.

Not that modern anthropologists or biologists have a better answer.

Over the past twenty years or so, the *Journal of Human Evolution* has mulled the question in a series of articles by P. E. Wheeler. He has boiled it down to a couple of questions:

Did we stand upright before or after we lost our hair?

Did we migrate from the forest to the savannah before or after we lost our hair?

Reviewing Wheeler's research in a 1996 *Journal of Human Evolution* article titled "Loss of Body Hair, Bipedality and Thermoregulation," Brazilian physicist Lia Quiroz do Amaral says, "Although it is widely accepted that naked skin facilitates dissipation of body heat, the circumstances favoring its evolution are quite unclear." Amaral concludes that "nakedness evolved in a more forested environment and possibly before or together with bipedality, not after it."

The *American Journal of Physical Anthropology* has followed a parallel path over the years in debating our loss of hair. In 1991 researchers Gary Schwartz and Leonard Rosenblum used allometry—relating the growth rate of one part of an organism to another part—to revisit some half-century-old research on primate hair. Their article, "The Allometry of Primate Hair Density and Evolution of Human Hairlessness," was an attempt to create a sequel to Darwin. "Distinctiveness of humans as the most hairless of primates poses a classic puzzle in evolutionary biology. Darwin considered that human

hairlessness was unlikely to have evolved purely by natural selection, as the absence of a reflective coat would
leave man unshielded from the intense rays of a tropical
sun." I will spare you the mathematical calculations. In
layman's terms: the bigger you are, the balder you aren't.
And the balder you aren't, the more you sweat. (You
knew that from college mixers.) They also concluded that
early humans had already lost their body fur before they
migrated from the forest to the grassland.

So not only do barbers owe those early Pliocene humans a debt of gratitude, so, too, do the manufacturers of
Ban, Sure, Secret, and Right Guard.

But we still don't know why we lost our hair.

Chapter 3

The World's Oldest (Legal) Profession

David Inman and Larry Magnes are sitting in an Indiana restaurant, discussing their barbershop histories. Larry grew up in the fifties in Paterson, New Jersey. Dave was raised in Jeffersonville, Indiana, in the sixties. Their youths were separated by a decade and half a continent, but when they get to talking barbershops, they have no trouble communicating.

LARRY: My first barber was Angelo. Angelo's was on the same block with the toy store and the drugstore and the hardware store. Angelo used to stand out front and you'd walk past on your way to the toy store and he'd say, "Hey kid, you need a haircut." Of course he could only cut hair one way. By my teens when I wanted something more stylish I switched to Hollywood Joe. Joe had all these pictures of these Italians stars on the wall. Hollywood stars but a lot of local stars, too. You know, guys in ruffled tux shirts. And he had Frankie Valli. You'd show Joe what you wanted from those pictures. He could cut a waterfall. He could cut a lot of different hairstyles. I got my first T.C. from Joe. T.C. stood for Tony Curtis. It was sort of a flattop on top and in the front he would take this mustache wax and make a little curl. When I wanted a Ducktail is when I started going to Joe. It was the beginning of the era of stylist as barber.

DAVE: My first barbershop was Russ and Don's on Maple Street in Jeffersonville, Indiana. They had a Coke machine in the back, with Cokes in the little bottles. You had a choice of Coke or Coke. That was it. And they had all those great barbershop magazines like *Field & Stream* and *True, the Men's Magazine*. And that container with blue liquid that they put combs in. Made you wonder what other people had in their hair. Russ had a strop on the side of his chair to sharpen his razor. And they used real hot lather on the back of your neck. I went in with my best friend Rodney Isrigg one time and because he was bigger they used the razor on him. They just used the clippers on me. And I was so jealous. My next barber was Bob Hill. I remember at Bob Hill's, the TV was always on. Bob gave me a haircut where *they comb* it straight forward and cut it. Bob had five barbers but it seemed only one was ever working. All the rest were outside smoking.

LARRY: The blue stuff that they kept combs in reminds me of Lilac Vegetale. It was this odd greenish color and you only saw it in barbershops. They would slap it on their hands and then rub it on the back of your neck after they shaved you.

DAVE: I left Bob Hill's to get my hair styled. It was five dollars more. The stylist who cut my hair tried to sell me shampoo in a bottle shaped like a Roman pillar. The cap was in the shape of some god's head.

LARRY: After Joe's I went to the Alexander Hamilton Hotel barbershop. They had firesticks that they would use and touch those stray hairs. So all your hair would be the same length but some would have a little ball on the end from being singed by the firestick.

DAVE: I tried a beauty shop. I remember people looking in the window at me. At that time you had to have a hot comb at home to keep your hair in shape between haircuts.

LARRY: In the early seventies you know the revolution had happened. I had gone from Angelo's to Hollywood Joe to the hotel and then to Rainy Day People. They burned incense and there were little burn spots on the counter from all the people who laid their hot roaches there. Everyone wore bell bottoms. I have curly hair and the barber asked if I wanted the natural look. I told him, "I'm in the National Guard," so he just sheared me like any other barber.

DAVE: The woman who cuts my hair now, I've been going to for ten years. She sort of took over when my old barber quit. Because I was handed off, it seemed to be kosher to switch to a woman.

There you have the history of the barbershop in America during the last half of the twentieth century. And all I had to do was sit a couple of guys down in an eatery, buy them burgers, bring up barbershops, and turn on the tape recorder. Their era, from 1950 to 2000, was a period that saw more turmoil in the barbering trade than any preceding time. During those fifty years the barbershop went from an every-other-week ritual to a monthly styling session. Women entered the trade in record numbers. Men left. Cutting became styling. But that's only the most recent half century. Barbering goes back a long way. And the only constant in barbering has been change.

The name barber comes from the Latin word *barba*, which means "Streisand." No, it means "beard," not the kind of beard who serves as a stand-in date so the paparazzi can't see who La Streisand is really dating, but the beard you find on a man's face. For barbers who spoke in their native Latin—and Latin has been a dead language for more millennia than I can remember—trimming the beard and shaving the face was an important part of the trade. The name barber has been around since Caesar. But there were barbers long before there was Latin (or Latin I or Latin II), long before there was the name barber.

Barbering isn't the oldest profession. But somebody had to cut hair to make sure the clients of the oldest profession looked presentable.

We don't know what the first haircut looked like. That's because the earliest cave drawings are imprecise. Okay, stick figures. We do know that those first haircuts were for function not fashion. If hair was an obstacle to outrunning a hungry saber-toothed tiger, if hair was catching on low-hanging limbs and causing Og to go from diner to dinner, then Og was going to cut it off using one of those fancy sharp-edged rocks that had just been invented: the prehistoric knife. Those rocks were used to scrape hair away from wounds and tan animal hides. But they were not used to give Og a Ducktail or a Flattop or a T.C. (*Spartacus*, which featured Tony Curtis wearing his T.C., was many millennia in the future.)

But sometime in prehistory Og or one of his relatives saw his own reflection in a pond and was sore afraid. Who was that ugly prehistoric person? Maybe Og scraped some hair off around the ears, making him look like a Neanderthal Billy Ray Cyrus. Or would that be a genetic redundancy? More likely some natural event caused Og to cut off his hair. Bangs were getting in his way while he painted stick figures on a cave wall. However it happened, one of our human ancestors cut his hair, some cave woman asked to touch it, and soon all his cave buddies were standing in line to borrow the sharp-edged stone.

According to *The Art and Science of Barbering*, a barbering textbook published in 1958, the earliest records of Egypt and China refer to some form of barbering. Wendy Cooper in her 1971 volume *Hair: Sex, Society, Symbolism* notes, "The street barber was common in Egypt; his customers would kneel at the side of the road while he shaved their heads." The Bible contains many references to this as well. As early as Genesis 41:14, and that's only forty chapters past "In the beginning," we find a Biblical note about barbering. When Joseph was summoned from his dungeon to see the pharaoh, he got a shave because he was afraid his beard would offend the Egyptian leader. In Ezekiel 5:1, God commands the prophet Ezekiel in the proper way of mourning: "And thou, son of man, take thee a sharp knife, take thee a barber's razor, and cause it to pass upon thine head and upon thy beard: then take thee balances to weigh, and divide the hair."

Of course the most famous Biblical barber was a hot number named Delilah. In Judges 16:17 her boyfriend Samson tells her, "A razor has never come on my head, for I have been a Nazarite to God from my mother's womb. If I am shaved, then my strength will leave me and I will become weak and be like any other man." You know what happened next. That was like a dare to Delilah. It's a sad story of love lost, freedom lost, and Samson bringing down the house, literally.

All these ancient barbers were something less than professional, itinerant workers who plied their craft catch-as-catch-can. Need a shave? Well, Izzie is down the street. Maybe you can catch him and he can shave you by the viaduct—running water and all that.

The barbershop—a fixed gathering spot for shaping up hirsute humans—was invented by the ancient Greeks. Greek historian Theoponipos, writing in the fourth century B.C., described those early shops. "Among the Tyrrhenians there are many shops for this purpose and well-trained staffs. . . . Persons enter these shops and let themselves be treated in any way on any part of the body without troubling about the looks of passersby."

So our street barber Izzie did his work in the open,

where getting a haircut could turn you into a public spectacle. The Greeks changed that by inventing the indoor barbershop. Barbers in ancient Greece were so popular that many took home good salaries. Juvenal writes of one who owned a number of villas. Martial knew a barber whose wife quickly moved up the social ladder because of his ability to bribe her way into society.

William Andrews, in his definitive 1904 haircutting history, *At the Sign of the Barber's Pole: Studies in Hirsute History*, writes, "[Barber] shops were general in Greece about 420 B.C., and then, as now, were celebrated as places where the gossips met. Barbers settled in Rome from Sicily in 299 B.C."

That's an event that's considered seminal by a number of barber historians: the arrival in Rome of Sicilian barbers. *The Textbook of Practical and Scientific Barbering*, published in 1947 by the Educational Department of the Journeymen Barbers, Hairdressers and Cosmetologists International Union of America, has the date a bit earlier but it also considers that ground zero for the development of the barbershop: "It is recorded that the first barbers were brought from Sicily to Rome in the year of 303 B.C. In the course of a few years they had so multiplied that the city was full of them." Its anonymous author also considers this date the origin of the barber's reputation as a gossip. "The barbershop soon became a common resort for loungers and idlers of every description. There the gossiping and inquisitive portion of the community came to receive the fashionable news and information regarding affairs of state. They came from the remotest corner of the city when hours of toil and business were over to discuss current politics." Sounds like Wib's place to me.

Barbershops arose to fill a need—and not just the need to gossip. The back fence was already around and could serve that purpose at a much smaller price. No, the barbershop arose because men were beginning to pay attention to their hair. *The Art and Science of Barbering* credits this to a desire by the common people to follow the lead of their more notable contemporaries. One early fashion leader was the Roman emperor Hadrian (A.D. 117–138) who grew a beard to cover his warts and scars, in the process creating a fashion for long, well-tended beards. A few centuries later the French king Charlemagne (A.D. 742–814) would set a fashion for long hair in his country.

Early barbers were more than just cutters of hair and shavers of beards; they were our first HMOs. It was not long into the first millennium (*The Art and Science of Barbering* sets it at A.D. 110) that barbers expanded their practice into surgery. The doctors of the Dark Ages were the monks and priests; they were the most learned people so the job fell to them. And they used barbers as their assistants. Today it may seem barbaric to have a barber perform surgery, but at the time it must have seemed like a good idea. In fact it was allowed to continue for almost 1,700 years. It's not a bad idea if you think about it: barbers had the tools (sharp pointy instruments), they knew human anatomy (they still have to study it in barber college today), and people didn't know all that much about surgery anyway.

Barbers in A.D. 110 were not removing gall bladders and performing nose jobs. They were pulling teeth, letting blood, and burning skin. And cutting hair. Long before Dr. Joseph Lister discovered the importance of sanitary surgery, barbers were concerned with having a clean shop. (Mayberry's Floyd wasn't the first prissy barber.) It was important to their customers; it was important to them.

France even sanctioned a barber's school of surgery in 1096. Soon after that barber-surgeons flourished in France and Germany. Andrews notes, "It is clear that in all parts of the civilised world, in bygone times, the barber acted as a kind of surgeon, or, to state his position more precisely, he practised phlebotomy, the dressing of wounds, etc." And from the twelfth century on barbers pretty much had the field to themselves. Up until then the clergy had cared for a person's soul and body, going so far as to practice medicine and surgery. Barbers frequently assisted monks in surgical procedures. But in 1163 Pope Alexander III in the Edict of Tours forbade clergy from surgery because it involved shedding blood, which the Pope felt was incompatible with the functions of the clergy. The clergy, however, were allowed to continue dispensing medicine. A parallel class of doctor-surgeons began to arise at about this time.

Freed to cut and bleed, barbers were soon acting as obnoxiously as personal injury lawyers in TV ads, going so far as to display containers of blood in their windows to advertise their bloodletting skills. It got so wide open that in 1307 London passed an ordinance requiring barbers to dispose of all that let-blood by having it "privately carried into the Thames under the pain of paying two shillings to the use of the Sheriffs."

Despite these nominal restrictions, barbers were riding high. The next year, 1308, Richard le Barber was named the first master of the Barbers' Company and sworn in at the Guildhall in London. In 1462, at the instigation of Edward IV, barbers were incorporated and given a Royal Charter. In 1540, the group was renamed the Company of Barber-Surgeons. Barbers and surgeons were united in one guild. Neither was exactly ecstatic about this, particularly the surgeons. They thought barbers were quacks—pretty strong stuff from guys for whom bloodletting was the height of civilized medical care. So during the reign of Henry VIII (1509–1547) Parliament passed a new law: "No person using any shaving or barbery in London shall occupy any surgery, letting of blood, or other matter, except of drawing teeth." Barbers could still be dentists but no longer could they be one-stop shopping for the shaggy, sick, and afflicted.

Barbers continued their quackery in what TV weathermen now call outlying areas but the end was in sight. Even with their diminished duties, barbers were still men of social import. During the reign of Queen Elizabeth (1558–1603), according to Andrews, "The rich families from the country thought it no disgrace . . . take rooms above some barber's shop." Can you imagine her namesake, the current Queen Elizabeth, taking a holiday and putting up for the night above a barbershop?

The barbershop itself was not unlike Floyd's neigh-
borly little establishment in Mayberry. Floyd had his radio, or, on occasion, Andy Griffith and his guitar. Andrews
says barbershops of the sixteenth century had their music. "A gittern, or guitar, lay on the counter, and this was
played by a customer to pass away the time until his turn
came to have his hair trimmed, his beard starched, his
mustachios curled, and his love-locks tied up."

Even then barbers were trying to sell their customers
up, not letting them settle for a simple trim but encour-
aging a stylish (and more expensive) 'do. The English
writer Robert Greene's allegory *A Quip for an Upstart
Courtier*, published in 1592, gives us a glimpse into a barber's chair-side sales technique. A nobleman sits in the
chair and the barber begins:

"Sir, will you have your worship's hair cut after the
Italian manner, short and round, and then frounst with
the curling irons to make it look like a half-moon in a
mist; or like a Spaniard, long at the ears and curled like
the two ends of an old cast periwig; or will you be
Frenchified with a love-lock down to your shoulders,
whereon you may wear your mistress's favour? The English cut is base, and gentlemen scorn it; novelty is dainty.
Speak the word, sir, my scissors are ready to execute your
worship's will."

A customer at that time would spend a couple of hours
having his hair combed and dressed and frounst. Then the
barber would address the noble's beard. Would his lord-
ship "have his peak cut short and sharp, and amiable like

an inamorata, or a broad pendent like a spade, to be amorous as a lover or terrible as a warrior and soldier; whether he will have his crates cut low like a juniper bush, or his subercles taken away with a razor; if it be his pleasure to have his appendices primed, or his moustachios fostered to turn about his ears like vine tendrils, fierce and curling, or cut down to the lip with the Italian lash—and with every question a snip of the scissors and a bow?"

As you can see barbers then, as now, were nothing if not talky.

Comenii Orbis Sensualium Pictus, known in the English-speaking world as *The Visible World,* was the first illustrated schoolbook and reveals that in 1658 the barber was still a surgeon in many parts of the globe. Accompanying an illustration of a barber drawing blood is this caption: "The Barber in the Barbers shop, cutteth off the hair and the Beard with a pair of Sizurs or shaveth with a Razor which he taketh out of his Case. And he washeth one over a Bason, with Suds running out of a Laver and also with Sope and wipeth him with a Towel, combeth him with a Comb and curleth him with a Crisping Iron. Sometimes he cutteth a Vein with a Pen-knife, where the blood spirteth out."

The barber as surgeon had been a long time in the making and the profession was very resistant to change, even if dictated by Parliament. As late as 1727, fable writer John Gay would describe a barber letting blood in "The God Without a Beard":

His pole, with pewter basins hung,
Black, rotten teeth in order strung,
Rang'd cups that in the window stood,
Lin'd with red rags, to look like blood,
Did well his threefold trade explain,
Who shavd, drew teeth, and breath'd a vein.

That would end soon. The official date for the complete separation of barbers and surgeons is generally considered to be 1745. France had separated the two a couple of years earlier with a decree by Louis XV prohibiting barbers from practicing surgery. But the final severing (so to speak) came when England's Parliament, at the urging of George II, passed a similar act in 1745. And that's why you can't get an appendectomy at the barbershop today.

Floyd the barber on *The Andy Griffith Show* might occasionally threaten Goober for calling his establishment a "clip joint" but in seventeenth- and eighteenth-century barbershops insults were taken seriously. There were even laws forbidding idle talk and requiring offenders to pay fines, known then as forfeits.

Shakespeare refers to this in *Measure for Measure* (Act V, Scene 1): ". . . The strong statutes stand like the forfeits in a barber's shop, as much in mock as mark." Particularly egregious was talk of cutting throats, the Shakespearean equivalent of joking about hijacking at an airport security counter.

Most rules, however, were good-natured, albeit strictly enforced. Andrews says the regulations were posted on the wall, "in a conspicuous manner, and might be read while the customer was awaiting his turn for attention at the hands of the knight of the razor. Forfeits had to be paid for such offences as the following: For handling the razors, for talking of cutting throats, for calling hair-powder flour, for meddling with anything on the shop-board." Andrews found a table of forfeits in a 1765 volume of forgotten lore by one Dr. Kenrick who claimed to have seen the list many years before in a Yorkshire town.

> *First come, first served—then come not late,*
> *And when arrived keep your sate;*
> *For he who from these rules shall swerve*
> *Shall pay his forfeit—so observe.*
> *Who enters here with boots and spurs*
> *Must keep his nook, for if he stirs*
> *And gives with arm'd heel a kick,*
> *A pint he pays for every prick.*
> *Who rudely takes another's turn*
> *By forfeit glass—may manners learn.*
> *Who reverentless shall swear or curse*
> *Must beg seven hapence from his purse.*
> *Who checks the barber in his tale,*
> *Shall pay for that a gill of yale;*
> *Who will or cannot miss his hat*
> *Whilst trimming pays a pint for that.*
> *And he who can but will not pay*

Shall hence be sent half-trimmed away;
For will he—nill he—if in fault,
He forfeit must in meal or malt.
But mark, the man who is in drink
Must the cannikin, oh, never, never clink."

Standard operating procedure at a barbershop was recognized even then as the subject for humor. I can easily imagine one of the wags at Wib's calling hair powder flour. As Shakespeare said, "as much in mock as mark."

Perhaps the forfeit system was a way to make up for the loss in surgical income. One thing is for sure: the falling of the curtain on the institution of the barber-surgeon brought hard times to the barbering profession. According to *The Art and Science of Barbering,* "Between 1750 and 1850 barbers had their roughest time. Beard trimming was not widely practiced. Whiskers became the vogue. The barbers resorted to wig making during this period."

The history of barbers in America is sketchy before the Civil War. Barbers may have crossed the Atlantic with Columbus but the respect they commanded on the continent didn't cross with them. *The Textbook of Practical and Scientific Barbering* notes, "Long hours, miserable compensation, cheap, unfair competitive prices continued to maintain barbering as a secondary occupation, and the inhuman shop conditions brought public consideration toward the barber to a minimum."

But this terrible time was about to end. Continues *The Textbook,* "To cope with these deplorable conditions, forts were made to re-establish the barbering profession in its place of historical importance and respectability. With this as its goal, on November 5, 1887, in Buffalo, New York, an organization of barbers was formed which is today known as the Journeymen Barbers, Hairdressers and Cosmetologists' International Union of America."

The Golden Age of barbering was at hand. Barbers all over the world would no longer be a ragtag bunch but professionals with professional guidelines and professional manners. Plus the ability to strike. All they lacked was professional training and that, too, was on the way. In 1893 Albert B. Moler founded the first barber college in Chicago. Before Moler, barbers learned through an apprenticeship, the same way lawyers and many other trades did. So your barber was only as good as his master. Moler changed all that with standardized training methods and a standardized textbook, which he wrote (and sold for a dollar).

Next came state barber laws. The first was passed in 1897 by the Minnesota legislature requiring that barbers be licensed. (Not trained, just licensed—a license based on a training course would come later.)

By 1956 Sherman Trusty, barber-author of *The Art and Science of Barbering*, could boast about fifty years of advancement by his trade. "Barbers have made tremendous progress, especially in the last half century. Instead of filthy hang-outs where only men gathered to exchange stories and have their beards trimmed, the modern barber shop is really an inviting parlor where scientific services are rendered. To early barbers, such services as

shampoos, tonics, facials, and scalp treatments were un-
known. The atmosphere of the barbershop now compares with that of the best professions." He also listed
other factors that had helped to make barbering more
professional: "Starting of the Terminal System, New York
City, 1916. Emphasis was placed upon sanitation in a way
to attract the attention of patrons.

"The revival of women's haircutting, about 1920. This
resulted in making men more conscious of their hair.

"Higher caliber of men entered barbering. They re-set
the atmosphere of the barbershop. Parents now allow
their children to visit a shop unaccompanied.

"Founding of the Associated Master Barbers Organization on November 19, 1924, in Chicago, Illinois.

"Founding of State associations of barber schools."

While Trusty was boasting about an unlimited future
for barbering, four young lads were tuning their instruments over in Liverpool, England. And barbering was
about to change again.

Herb Pierce, who's been circling the chair at Xavier
Nalley's Barbershop in Saint Matthews, Kentucky, since
1958, can tell you the exact day that barbering changed.
It was February 7, 1964: the day the Beatles' plane
touched down in New York City. "The Beatles created a
depression in barbering," mourns Pierce.

"The Beatles hurt me more than the hippies," adds my
barber, Wib Scarboro. No other event shaped the future
of barbering the way that one plane ride from Liverpool
to LaGuardia did. The impact wasn't immediate. Pierce

says it took till 1968 before the effect took hold. "A lot of kids, their parents wouldn't let them wear their hair long at first. But it took off in a big way in '68. From then to '74 it was hard."

I was one of those kids Pierce was talking about; my mother couldn't bear the thought of me with Beatles hair. She was just getting used to the Flattop. But I went along with the fashion breeze. The day the Beatles landed, I had a Flattop. Within six months I had what my high school friend Richard Arnold called a Julius Caesar cut (he had one, too). We let our Flattops grow out, but not out too much. Maybe two inches. Then we combed the hair straight forward. We were still close-cropped on the side. But my barbershop habits were changing. I didn't go every two weeks like clockwork anymore. I would wait until my father told me I was going to need dog tags pretty soon if I didn't get a haircut.

When I was a senior in college, I quit going to the barbershop altogether. On June 2, 1969, my parents arrived in town for my college graduation: they didn't recognize me. My mother cried that night. It was the third hairstyle of mine that she had cried over. I didn't go to the barber again for a decade.

Pierce says he figured it out once, how hard barbers were hit in that decade from 1968 to 1978. "The state of Kentucky lost about two thousand barbers. Dropped from five thousand to three thousand. For every four barbers that quit, a barbershop closed. A lot of barbers got out of it back then." Many never to return. It was during this hair-cutting depression that many barbershops became styling salons. And old-time barbers don't cotton much to the stylists. "We don't do foo-foo in barbering," says Jo Ann Blake, a barber in Jeffersonville, Indiana. "We cut hair."

Even at its lowest point, when every young man seemed to have shoulder length hair, Pierce knew it would get better again. His old barber college teacher John McCue had told him. "He retired in '79 after fifty years of barbering and he had seen it all. He said hair was like clothes. He said it all came full circle. When he started out in the twenties, the style was long and full. Then the regular haircut came in. After the war it was all short hair. If you couldn't cut short hair then, you couldn't barber. Then finally it came back to full hair."

Sure enough hairstyles headed around the circle in the late seventies, and it was music again that turned the tide on long hair. John Travolta sported a shorter 'do in the wildly popular disco movie *Saturday Night Fever* and soon disco dance floors were flooded with mid-length pompadours (and white suits and open shirts). It was a complicated haircut—Travolta's character never wanted anyone touching his hair—and it accelerated the move back to hair stylists.

The conservative Reagan years brought back conservative haircuts. The worst hair trend of that era was popularized in the movie *Greed,* in which Wall Street guru Gordon Gekko (Michael Douglas) sported a combed-back style that harked back thirty years to the days of greasy kid stuff.

The nineties saw hair getting shorter in most quarters. But there was also an anything-goes mood about hair. Today you can walk down the street and see just about anything on a man's head, from a Flattop to a ponytail to a bad toupee.

With so many styles out there, men have been turning more and more to the aptly named stylists. If my computer search was right—and it probably wasn't, but it was close enough—at 10:57 A.M. on December 12, 1999, there were 55,893 barbershops left in the United States. The use of the word *left* implies there used to be more. There were. Memory alone tells you that. But if you want some cold, hard statistics, the 1950 U.S. Retail Census lists 287,655 barbershops. That's a big drop from more than a quarter million in 1950 to a little more than fifty thousand at the turn of the century.

The circle may have come back to short hair but several thousand barbers aren't around to see it. And the ones who are still around haven't forgotten the hard times.

My barber, Wib Scarboro, sums it up: "Once my son asked to borrow twenty bucks; he wanted to buy a Beatles' record. I said, 'You got to be kidding. They caused me to starve for about ten years.'"

Chapter 4

The First Time

The little boy in the chair is wincing, shaking his head back and forth, and rubbing his nose, in general making it nearly impossible for Russell Hiatt to cut his hair. But Hiatt has a steady hand and a gentle manner that wins the tyke over. Soon the small boy is climbing down off that high pedestal, digging joyfully through the lollipop bowl and looking quizzically at the paper that Russell has handed him: "First Haircut Certificate."

First Haircut Certificate

This is to certify that...

_____

has bravely met all of the requirements of receiving his first haircut and has graduated from babyhood on the _____ day of _____ in the year of _____

Ceremonies took place at:

_____
_____

_____
Authorized Signature

The first haircut acquires mythic status over time. It was a great day in your life. You forget about the screaming fit, about the pull of the razor's whirring blades, about the barber's not-so-gentle hands.

Ask barbers about first haircuts and you get an entirely opposite reaction. First haircuts are a pain; sometimes they are even painful. Every barber has the story of the little boy who bit him or the mother who grabbed up her baby and raced out screaming.

Barber's manuals over the years have recognized the "special circumstances" of cutting a kid's hair. Sherman Trusty, in his 1958 manual, *The Art and Science of Barbering*, got straight to the point in his section on "Boys' Hair Cuts":

"Point of inestimable value, put the boy at ease. Speak to him softly and nicely. Ask him something about himself, such as 'do you like trains?' or 'where do you go to school?'"

Trusty's trusty advice continues, "If the electric clipper frightens the child, try the hand clipper. Sometimes, showing the child the clipper drives fear away. Be on your guard and ever-ready to remove implements from the child's head."

What he's saying there is: watch out for bubble gum wads lodged in the hair overnight.

Trusty says barbers should be especially considerate of the child's escort. He says to ask the parent, not the child, what kind of haircut to give. "And never slight a child's cut. Any defects in cut will likely be noticed by the escort

or parents and meet with instant disapproval." The trans-
lation here is: if you don't do a good job, the parents are
going to yell at you.

Most barbers hate cutting a toddler's hair.

But not Russell Hiatt. Hiatt specializes in it.

"People come from all over the South with their little
boys. I get grandfathers come in here, tell me I give them
their first haircut, give their boy his first haircut and now
they want me to give their grandson his first haircut. Had
a fellow in here yesterday from Gastonia tell me that exact tale."

Russell Hiatt didn't always enjoy the task. "When I first
started, these older barbers would head out as soon as a
mama brought her little boy in. They knew how to get out
the back door. I learned later how to go to the drugstore."

Russell Hiatt owns City Barbershop in Mount Airy,
North Carolina. It's the shop he started in back in 1946.
But Mount Airy is more than just Mount Airy. And City
Barbershop is more than just City Barbershop. It's listed
in the phone book as City Barbershop. But painted on
the front window is this: FLOYD'S CITY BARBERSHOP.

Andy Griffith grew up in Mount Airy. When he went to
Hollywood and became famous as the sheriff of fictional
Mayberry, North Carolina, he sketched little details from
his childhood into the show. And one of them was the local barbershop. It was Floyd's on TV. It was City Barbershop in Mount Airy, until the local arts council repainted
the sign in his window and added the name Floyd's, as a
tourism thing.

And Russell is Floyd, sort of. "When Andy lived in Mount Airy there were six barbers here. All of us cut his hair at one time or another. None of us were named Floyd. Andy probably took all six of us and made a Floyd. I have people tell me I look like Floyd and talk like Floyd." And that connection has people dropping in to City Barbershop all day long, just to look around.

But long before the Floyd's craze, Russell Hiatt made a name cutting kids' hair. "Many a kid has got his first haircut here." It started by accident; the older barbers would take a flyer when a kid came in, leaving good old Russell to cut the kid's head. Then he started taking pictures of the kids and putting them on the wall. Soon he was taking pictures of everybody who got a haircut. Then everybody who came in the shop. "I have eighteen thousand to nineteen thousand pictures on the wall. I could have one-hundred thousand. If somebody comes and says I took their picture years ago, if they tell me when they were here, I can find them."

He heard about another fellow, a barber, who passed out First Haircut Certificates. So he worked up his own design and had a few printed up. And a few more. "Thousands over the years. They say they're hanging in houses all over the South."

Russell Hiatt doesn't cut as much hair as he used to. He's earned the rest—he turned seventy-seven in 2000. But he'll still cut a little boy's hair on request. And he still comes in the shop every day, or every day it's open, which is everyday except Sunday and Wednesday. But he's turned most of the haircutting duties over to Donna.

"She's been with me fourteen years all total. She's my niece. Can't find male barbers anymore."

Russell mostly sits in his chair. "Donna cuts; I'm more the master of ceremonies."

When Hancel Woods moved back to his old hometown—and my old hometown—in 1997, he decided to revisit his old barbershop, Paul Lewis's Barbershop on Main Street. "I told him I used to get my hair cut there, that I climbed up on the board and he gave me my first haircut. He pointed at the corner and said, 'There's that board, right over there.' And a cold chill went down my back. That was my childhood."

Hancel dragged his brother-in-law Bruce Haney along for moral support. And to get a haircut.

Even though Hancel's and Bruce's combined ages top hundred, Mr. Lewis insisted on calling them "boys," as in, "You boys have a seat and I'll get to you in a jiffy."

After introductions Ray Garland, the customer in the chair, gave Hancel a wink. "I knowed your daddy. I sold him a double-barreled Stevenson Model 311 shotgun years ago. I'd traded a long-nosed dog for that gun. That dog's nose was so long it looked like he had an extra nose."

Garland reflected on the years he spent working on the Clinchfield Railroad (he retired in 1977) while Mr. Lewis snip, snip, snipped away. Bruce and Hancel each got a haircut from Mr. Lewis. Bruce would later recall, "I was somewhat concerned, watching him cut Hancel's hair, because he closes his eyes as he talks and cuts—and I thought for a minute we had wandered into a blind man's barbershop. Actually, he did a darn good job, and only charged us six bucks."

Mr. Lewis was in an expansive mood today, talking about his girlfriend. He admitted to having cut hair in the same location for forty years but he wouldn't admit to his age. "I got me a thirty-eight-year-old girlfriend and I don't want her to know."

Mr. Lewis took his time with his refound customers, rejoicing in the memories they brought with them.

Hancel didn't wince or flinch or squirm like he did the first time he sat for Mr. Lewis all those years ago. He noted that the chair seemed a little tighter than he remembered it. "Seat hasn't changed in forty years," noted Mr. Lewis.

As the clippers hummed and the conversation continued, Hancel kept glancing over at that worn-out old
plank, the one he sat on so many times in his youth. "I remember the day Mr. Lewis moved me down off the
board and into the regular seat. That was a big day in my
young life. I didn't know what a rite of passage was at the
time but that was my first one."

The board leaned in the corner, waiting for the next kid.

Chapter 5

Name That Mane

Passing a middle-aged man on the street sporting an out-dated pompadour reminded me of a fall afternoon forty years earlier. My best friend on the basketball team, Jerry Harmon, and I were sitting in the locker room before basketball practice, when in strutted a straggler from gym class. "Check that hood," said Jerry, loud enough for me to hear but not loud enough to attract the attention of the hood. "Check that hair—a jelly roll with fenders." I almost fell off the bench laughing. I thought Jerry made it up; he was a clever guy. We were both sophomores and both benchwarmers that season—me more than him—and I can remember many of his bench comments.

But on this day I thought he had outdone himself: a jelly roll with fenders. That was exactly what it looked like. The top hair was combed forward into a mass that looked like the bow of a ship. The center top had been patted down carefully to form walls. Then the sides had been swept back in a style that looked like a Buick's fenders.

It was later in the year that I learned that was the official name for the hood's haircut: a Jelly Roll with Fenders.

It was a gorgeous style that must have taken hours to cut and more hours to reshape each morning. And it was popular with the budding juvenile delinquents who gathered around the motorcycle stand each morning at my high school.

Over the years there have been plenty of contenders for the title of Greatest Haircut.

At the top of the list is a haircut invented by a guy with a contender kind of name: Joey Cirello. Cirello, a South Philadelphia barber, was the guy who created the D.A. haircut. Okay, D.A. isn't a very exciting haircut name. But that was the polite-company abbreviation.

What Joe Cirello invented, noodling around on the hair of a blind orphan boy who hung out at his shop, was a cut called the Duck's Ass (usually called the Ducktail when Mom was around).

The name is a perfect description. Cirello piled teenagers' hair high on top, then swirled the sides out and back so that they met in a perfect imitation of the business end of a duck.

Cirello came up with the design in 1939, after working a year and a half to perfect it. In 1979, on the occasion of the fortieth anniversary of the hairstyle, he told the *Philadelphia Inquirer*, "What I wanted was like a duck's ass, excuse my expression. It was just an idea I had, to do something different. All the other barbers thought I was crazy."

He didn't call it the D.A. He named it the Swing, after Benny Goodman's music. "The local high school kids started calling it the 'Duck's Ass' because of the wings on the sides and the point in the back," he told *Philadelphia* magazine in 1990. "I shortened it to D.A."

In 1986 he told *Esquire* that the D.A. style didn't come to him in a vision "as most people suspect" but from playing around with hair. "I probably never would have invented it if I had gone to barber school." He had learned haircutting at his uncle's knee in 1926, when he was eleven. He was a full-fledged barber by thirteen and had his own shop by age seventeen.

During World War II some friends dared him to enter the D.A. in a hairstyling contest at New York's Statler Hotel. To Cirello's surprise, he won. The D.A. was named Most Original Cut. The prize was a contract with Warner Bros. as a studio stylist.

The D.A. was a prizewinner but it didn't win any popularity contests—yet. War—and the G.I. haircut, a buzz named for its soldier look—intervened. The D.A. wouldn't sweep the country until the James Dean generation.

What propelled the D.A. into the lexicon was an accident of location. Cirello's shop was in South Philadelphia, home of the popular television teen dance party, *American Bandstand.* Some of the boys on the show frequented Cirello's shop. They adopted the D.A. and the rock and rollers who performed on the show noticed the style. Imitation begat imitation. Cirello told the *Philadelphia Inquirer,* "When the music managers started bringing their kids into the shop, we knew we were onto something."

Cirello also claimed to have invented the rattail, a tiny pigtail style popularized by little boys in Wal-Mart stores in the eighties. Shortly before his death in 1994 he revealed the secret he had kept for many years, of how he cut the D.A. "(Other barbers) didn't know how I cut the back," he told *Philadelphia* magazine. "I'd grease it with Wildroot Crème and butch wax and cut the center of the back, a canal, and comb the hair back into the canal. That was my secret."

The Ducktail was a descriptive name but haircuts have always had descriptive names. In *At the Sign of the Barber's Pole: Studies in Hirsute History* (1904), author

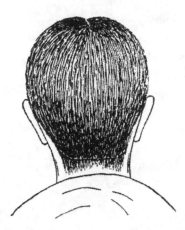

William Andrews refers to "the gentleman's cut, the common cut, the Court cut, and county cut."

Oftentimes the name of the styles referred to the wearer's country of origin. Sixteenth-century British writer Robert Greene in "Quip for an Upstart Courtier," notes hair cut in the "Italian manner," "Frenchified," "the English cut," even the "Italian lash."

But the labels could also refer to the wearer who made it popular. The bangs look was called the Caesar because it was popularized by Roman emperor Julius Caesar. Two millennia later the curly-bangs look was called the T.C. because it was popularized by Tony Curtis as a cute little slave boy in the Roman epic *Spartacus*. Five years later the T.C. was replaced in the popular imagination by the Beatles' cut (also called the Mop-top).

Trusty's 1958 tome *The Art and Science of Barbering*

has ten illustrated pages of wonderful haircuts with wonderful haircut names: Butch, Boogie, Forward Boogie, Flat-Top Boogie, Waterfall, Cold Ducktail, Crewcut, Flat-Top, Forelock Flip, Shingle, Twirl.

Cars have always figured prominently in hairstyle names, from Fenders to the Camaro to the current style of close-shaved sides called Whitewalls.

But although popular hairstyles once came from military and political leaders, in the last half century it has been the music and movie industries that have inspired new 'do's.

It's always been young people who set hairstyles according to D.A. inventor Cirello. "Never go against the younger generation because they set the pace," he told *Esquire*. "It's always been like that and it won't ever change." So today

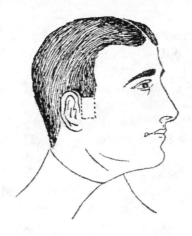

you can almost tell what kind of music a person listens to by the cut of his hair. Punk look—punk music. Pretty boy hair—pretty boy music. Fans of the country group Alabama look like the members of Alabama.

People use their hair to tell you about their lives. But that's nothing new either. Phillip Stubbes, a chronic complainer of the sixteenth century (he entitled his 1583 gripefest *Anatomie of Abuses*), believed your haircut was your message to the world. "When you come to be trimmed they will ask you whether you will be cut to look terrible to your enemy, or amiable to your friend; grim and stern in countenance, or pleasant and demure; for they have diverse kinds of cuts for all these purposes."

At this writing one of the most popular hairstyles in America is one you probably never thought about, since it's a good two decades old. But it, too, came out of the music culture.

Hairstylists call it the Bi-level. (Actually, they usually call it "awful," but when they use a name, they use the name Bi-level.)

Pop culture connoisseurs call it the Camaro (among many names).

But to the hundreds of thousands of young men who sport the 'do, it is simply the Mullet. The name comes from the 1967 Paul Newman film *Cool Hand Luke*. Dragline, the chain gang's self-appointed enforcer, calls a bunch of folks with shaggy hair "mullet heads." The dictionary hasn't yet caught up with hair fashion when it comes to the Mullet. It insists that a mullet is a fish.

For purposes of this book the Mullet is anything but a fish. It is the haircut that caught on in the eighties and never left—at least in certain neighborhoods.

How to describe it?

If you are familiar with country music, it is the hairdo sported—and popularized—by Billy Ray Cyrus. And for that reason many people call the Mullet the Achy-Breaky-Mistaky, after Cyrus's big hit "Achy Breaky Heart."

The Mullet goes straight back from the sideburn, then drops precipitously behind the ear so that it is short in front and long in the back. That's why some call it the 7—for the shape of the hair, and why others call it the 10-90—the percentage of hair on top compared to the percentage on the bottom.

Those who call it the Camaro do so because its owners seem to drive Camaros. That's why it is also called El Camino in other neighborhoods.

It's also called the Kentucky Waterfall (for the precipitous drop), the Tennessee Tophat (because of its popularity among country music lovers), the Mudflap (that's also what it looks like), the Ape Drape (very descriptive name, that), the Whorehouse (business in the front, party in the back), the Schlong (short and long), the Soccer Rocker (because of its popularity among soccer players), and, my favorite, Hockey Hair (watched any NHL games lately?).

Some Mullet wearers go so far as to perm the long part—the Curly Mullet—and then pull it back in a ponytail (which gives us its derivative, the Pony Mullet).

The modern Mullet is more than a haircut; it's a way of life. You can spot it at the state fair: the whole family walking around, Daddy Mullet, Momma Mullet, Johnny Mullet, all in tank tops and acid-washed jeans, scarfing down corn dogs, one Mullet balancing a corn dog in one hand while fiddling with a cigarette lighter; Daddy Mullet anxious to get home so he can down his six-pack of Pabst.

Traveling a parallel if sometimes convergent path through the years have been the hair fashions of African-American men. Make no mistake, black men have always styled their hair in distinctive ways. Historian John Thornton, in his 1992 book *Africa and Africans in the Making of the Atlantic World: 1400–1680*, traces this love of hairstyle all

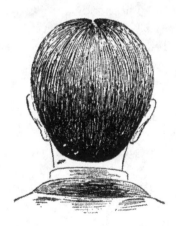

the way back to Africa. "When Europeans first came into contact with western Africa in the late fifteenth century they commented on the myriad hairstyles worn by the people they met." A drawing from Pieter de Marees's 1602 book *Description and Historical Account of the Gold Kingdom of Guinea* shows eight African men with eight different hairstyles, from a shaved head to a side braid to what might even be early cornrows.

These varying styles carried over to early slave culture in this country. When architect Benjamin Latrobe visited Virginia in 1797, he noted in his sketchbook that one black man had "taken his hair out of a twist" and another black man with "impressively sculpted hair begins combing and pulling the wool of the Man on the tub till he has compleated the Coiffure."

Eighteenth-century runaway slave ads describe a wide

variety of hairstyles, according to Shane White and Graham White in the 1998 scholarly study *Stylin': African American Expressive Culture from Its Beginnings to the Zoot Suit*. They note that most ads refer to long bushy hair but others mention hair cut short, combed, parted, even shaved off. They conclude, "Most slaveholders in the British mainland colonies seem to have allowed African Americans to style their hair as they pleased."

There even appear to have been regional variations, much like today. In *A History of the Public Markets of the City of New York*, published in 1862, antiquarian Thomas de Voe describes the blacks who came to breakdown (dancing) contests at Catharine Slip: "The New Jersey blacks, mostly from Tappan, wore their forelocks plaited with tea leaves while the Long Island blacks had their hair in a queue tied with a dried eel skin."

But in the nineteenth century that changed. Shane White and Graham White found few mentions of hairstyle in runaway slave ads and the few that did noted short hair. They confirmed this by studying slave photographs from the 1850s.

Short hair seems to have carried through into the twentieth century. White and White say this was so because, "The early years of freedom opened relatively few opportunities for aesthetic expression, and ahead lay a racial climate so oppressive that any sign of ostentation would have been perilous."

Style returned to African-American hair in the first years of the twentieth century with the invention of hair straighteners. One popular variation of the straightening process was developed by Indianapolis businesswoman Sarah Breedlove McWilliams Walker, who used the professional name of Madam C. J. Walker. But hers was not the only product on the market. An ad in a 1903 edition of the black newspaper, the *St. Louis Palladin,* touted the "Wonderful Discovery Ford's Original Ozonized Ox Marrow. Curly Hair Made Straight by this wonderful hair pomade. . . . It is the only sure preparation in the world that makes kinky or curly hair straight. Do not be misled by substitutes that claim to be just as good. 50 cents a bottle. Full directions with every bottle. From Chicago."

Straightening hair began a style that has its devotees today: what Malcolm X in his autobiography called the "conk." Malcolm X even describes his introduction to the style. A friend named Shorty mixed up a homemade version—a concoction of eggs, mashed potatoes, and lye—then poured this foul-smelling potion onto Malcolm's hair with painful, but successful, results.

This style went by many names—conk, process, marcel—and it went everywhere. Cab Calloway wore it. So did Nat "King" Cole, Sammy Davis Jr., and Louis Armstrong. You still see it.

Harvard professor and black intellectual Henry Louis Gates Jr. in his 1996 memoir *Colored People,* noted the continued popularity of hair straightening today: "It's a wonder we don't have a national holiday for Madam C. J. Walker . . . rather than for Dr. King."

Gates admits to having spent much of his youth trying

to straighten his own hair. "Straight just means not kinky, no matter what contours the curl might take. Of the wide variety of techniques and methods I came to master almost all had two things in common: a heavy, oil-based grease and evenly applied pressure."

He says he tried them all, "from sea-blue Bergamot, to creamy vanilla Duke to the godfather of grease, the formidable Murray's. Now, Murray's was some serious grease. Whereas bergamot was like oily Jell-O and Duke was viscous and sickly sweet, Murray's was light brown and hard." His father used to say of Murray's: "Hard as lard and twice as greasy."

As the sixties dawned, most black men wore their hair either short or straightened. That would soon change. The Civil Rights movement brought a return to a natural look. In *Hair Raising*, her 1996 treatise on beauty, culture, and African Americans, Noliwe M. Rooks says, "As the civil

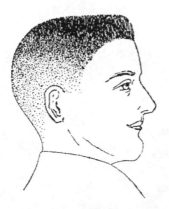

rights movement became the black liberation or black power movement. . . . wearing an Afro became synonymous with nationalist sentiments." Hair politics. But politics soon became fashion. There were now three choices for African-American men: straight, short, and tall. Some were very tall. Professional basketball player Artis Gilmore had an Afro crown that made him seem even taller than his already imposing seven feet. David Vish, who watched Gilmore in his years with the Kentucky Colonels, swears his Afro touched the rim, which is set at ten feet.

Like Newton's apple, what goes up must come down. Afros began shrinking and in the eighties they were supplanted by the African-American version of the Mullet: Jheri curls, a behind-the-ears ringlets style that got its name from Jheri Curl, the hair-care product used to give the curls their sheen.

In the nineties, African-American hairstyles, too, went

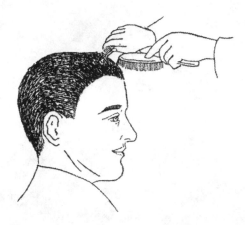

in divergent directions. Many athletes affected the bald look popularized by NBA superstar Michael Jordan, who shaved his head in part to compensate for a retreating hairline.

Cornrows, a style of short braids pleated into neat paths, also found their followers. At this writing you can walk down a city street and see a limitless array of hairstyles: shaved, short, short on top and shaved on the side (the Fade), short Afros, unkempt Afros, braids, locks, cornrows, even—yes—a process.

The Mullet is not the most horrible haircut in history. It's on the list, certainly, but there are other contenders for this title. Here's my Top Ten Horrible Haircuts in History (in chronological order), compiled after discussions with barbers all over the country. Call it my Barber Poll:

1. *The Caesar* Bangs forward, a halo of leaves covering the top.
   Julius Caesar wove ivy into his hair to hide his receding hairline.
2. *The Pepys* Full and girly-curly.
   Samuel Pepys sported the biggest mass of curls in the English-speaking world and he fretted for weeks on end in his famous diaries about his hair—keep it short? Let it grow long? Wear a wig? Wear a periwig? If Shirley Temple had been an obese middle-aged English diarist she would have had Samuel Pepys's hair.
3. *The Washington* First in war, first in peace, and last in the barber chair.
4. *The Napoleon* Charge to the front.
   Napoleon conquered the world—or a large part of it—but he could never conquer those unruly bangs. And, frankly, bangs are just not attractive on men. Please pass the word on to Bill Gates, whose own bangs may reveal an identification with Napoleon.
5. *Albert Einstein* Early fright wig.
   Okay, Albert Einstein was the smartest man in the world. But did that give him license to eschew personal grooming? Einstein sported the original Don King look.
6. *Porter Wagoner* Comb it high, high, high.

In the fifties there were two famous pompadours: Elvis's and Porter Wagoner's. Elvis had a great pompadour, perfectly suited for his face and for his style. His cut was cool. Wagoner, whose hair swept up higher and farther back than Elvis's, was the exact opposite. His hair was not cool. The pomp combined with his flamboyant cowboy shirts shouted, "I'm out of it." When he was still modeling the same haircut a quarter century later, it was just sad.

7. *That Guy, in Flock of Seagulls* Every bad hairstyle combined into one.

Flock of Seagulls was a British New Wave band of the 1980s. Its members are remembered today not for their music (they had one hit) but for their ridiculous hair—emphatically teased tresses that belied the fact that two band members were hairdressers. "That Guy" was group founder and hairdresser (!!!) Mike Score. His cascading bleach-blond locks combined the worst parts of the Pompadour with the Mohawk, the Jelly Roll, the Ducktail, and a windy day.

8. *Lou Henson* Living in fear of the wind.

New Mexico State basketball coach Lou Henson has America's worst comb-over. He takes hair that rightfully belongs in his sideburns, grows it to Beatles length, then combs it over to cover a shiny pate. Wouldn't you love to see him coming out of the pool?

9. *ZZ Top* Haute homeless.

It's hard to believe that rockers ZZ Top had a hit

with "Sharp-Dressed Man." This three-dude rock collective is the exact opposite of sharp when it comes to hairstyle. The bookend guys have adopted hair and beards that just grow and grow with nothing to check them, and the guy in the middle prefers that curly swept-back hair last spotted in Vegas lounges in the seventies.

10. *Pete Rose* Leads the league in Bad Hair.
I have no opinion on whether his gambling habit should keep Pete Rose out of baseball's Hall of Fame. But if the committee wants another reason, here it is: ban him for a career of bad hair. In a sport notorious for being light years behind the times in hair fashion, Pete stands alone. The Flattop went out in the mid-sixties; Pete wore it into middle age. A full decade after the Beatles introduced the Moptop to America, Pete let his hair grow. But not into something stylish. No, he opted for the Jimmy Connors Flop-top. And when his gambling world came crashing down on his career, the fifty-year-old former star went to his belligerent press conference with the spiked hairstyle of a teenager. If you haven't seen Pete lately, seek him out. He can often be spotted in his south Florida eatery Pete Rose's Ball Park Café. He's the stocky guy with the prematurely orange hair.

At my high school reunion a couple of years ago I saw Jerry Harmon. It was like we stepped back in time thirty years to those bygone days riding the pine, watching the starters get the minutes. "Look at that guy over there," he said.

It was the same guy—Mr. Jelly Roll with Fenders. The Jelly Roll was gone, moved down to a belly roll. But he still had the swept-back sides—"Bald Guy with Fenders," Jerry said.

Chapter 6

A Barbershop
by Any Other Name...
Would Still Smell Like Lucky Tiger

The bank's only open two days a week in Buford, Georgia. That's the kind of town it is.

Hanging in there two blocks from the bank, on the railroad side of the street, I visited a tired little clip joint. In the shop, off to the side, are arranged an assortment of hair-care products: shampoos, crèmes, rinses. And there, next to the Lucky Tiger hair tonic, is a bottle I haven't seen in thirty years. Sur-Lay, it reads.

It looks the same, it smells the same. I have to buy it. It's a bargain even at $5.15.

You see, Sur-Lay was my father's hair tonic, and by extension, my own, as a boy.

Sur-Lay was pronounced almost like the woman's name Shirley, by my father anyway. It was as if Shirley were French, and it came out Shur-Lay. It was a wonderful, exotic-sounding name for what was essentially colored, scented alcohol water.

Sur-Lay was—and still is—reddish in color with a unique aroma. It smells like my father. It has a crisp, biting odor with notes of cherry and whorehouse. It is one of the oldest smells in my life, sniffed while riding on my father's shoulders.

My father kept it on the floor under the commode, in the back near the wall, and I can remember watching him reach for it in the morning after he'd finished shaving. He'd pour a thimbleful into his hand and then rub it through his hair till it glistened.

Sur-Lay lived up to its name; it gave his hair a sure lay. It would have taken a hurricane to move my father's hair out of place. I know that because as soon as he had rubbed the tonic into his hair, he would pour another splat into his hand and rub it into my hair. Then he would lift me up and let me comb my hair in the mirror. I'd find the part line, ease the short hair down on the side, then bring the full hair straight across. I looked like Elvis with more manageable hair. So did my father. So did all the men in the neighborhood. The other boys? That was a another story. In the fifties the neighborhood boys were divided into two camps: Lance Harris, Tony Wampler, and I had Elvis hair; Mike Wampler, Donnie Jarvis, and Mike Jarvis, had G.I. hair.

Hairstyles were simple then: short or long. "Take a little off the top" or "Give me a G.I."

My father had that same hairstyle till the day he died in 1986. I have a picture of him from 1931, when he was a junior in high school, and his hair was the same even then: parted on the side, combed over, and pulled back a bit at the peak.

And all held in place by Sur-Lay.

Call it gel or tonic, pomade or mousse, it's all the same product in different wrappers. And it is older than the barbershop. The Ebers Papyrus, the ancient Egyptians' answer to drugstore.com, contains a recipe for a hair tonic. You wouldn't want to use it. (In fact, you couldn't make it unless you happened to have some moon root lying around the house.)

We have always been rubbing stuff in our hair and calling it hair tonic. In fact, the medicine cabinets and toiletry chests in African-American residences are also stocked with tonics and lotions, only the names are different. Instead of Vitalis, it's Murray's. Vitalis provides hold; Murray's relaxes. African Americans, too, have a long history with hair grease, dating back to the homemade hair straighteners of the nineteenth century.

Hair tonic was one of the most profitable items in barbershops at the turn of the century. Barbers made the tonics up themselves—or bought the stuff by the barrel—and dispensed it a teaspoon at a time for an "Osage Rub," a three-minute scalp massage that cost the barber less than a penny and the customer ten cents.

A. B. Moler, who wrote the first barber manual, provided formulas for hair tonics, including one for Tonic for a Dry Scalp. If this sounds like a drink they serve at the Waldorf bar, well, that's the way hair tonics were made—lots of alcohol.

TONIC FOR A DRY SCALP

Bay Rum	1 pint.
Witch Hazel	1 pint
Alcohol	1 pint
Glycerine	2 ozs.
Tincture of Cantharides	2 ozs.
Ammonia	½ oz.

Mix all together and filter.
For oily scalp, use 1 oz. of glycerine instead
of two.

(Cantharides is commonly known as Spanish fly. It is
compounded from the dried blister beetle and was considered the Viagra of its day, its day being when young
men in hot rods had fantasies about "hot dates." Ask your
local pharmacist about it and see if he laughs. What the
hell it's doing in hair tonic is a whole other question.)

Things were going swell in the early years of the twentieth century; barbers were making lots of money, customers had very hard hair, and then along came that
meddler Fred Fitch. Fitch, an Iowa farm boy turned barber, had built a small shampoo manufacturing empire but
he hadn't made a dent in the nation's collective scalp
problem. At the turn of the century lots of people com-
plained about their scalps itching. Check out newspapers

of the time for patent "scalp itch" remedies. Using old-fashioned trial and error research, Fitch figured out that the main ingredient in most hair tonics of the time, wood grain alcohol, wasn't a solution, but part of the problem, contributing to oily and itchy scalps. (Another part of the problem was that folks just didn't bathe all that frequently.) It was Fitch who convinced the government to include a clause in the landmark American Pure Food and Drug Act of 1906 that said "wood alcohol is condemned as a dangerous poison unfit for use in preparations intended for man or beast."

No longer could a barber whip up a vat of tonic in the back room. Now he had to buy approved tonics. So away went the barrel of tonic. And the barrel of profits.

Fred Fitch may have hurt the barber's bottom line but he also ushered in the golden age of hair tonic. Barbers began buying small bottles of commercially prepared hair dressings. This way they could extract a premium from the customer for a rub of exotic oil. At least the oils sounded exotic, even if most were just colored, scented alcohol. Excelsior Foaming Hair Tonic was a pale yellow rub. And grape-colored Eau de Quinine Hair Tonic came from Pinaud. There was the sumptuous-looking Healox Lavender Lotion and the crisp-feeling Westphal's Auxiliator for the Hair. Three Roses offered a cranberry-colored Hair Tonic for Loose Dandruff. Odell American Beauty was a minty-colored hair and scalp tonic with lanolin oil that was "stimulating, refreshing, dresses hair perfectly, removes loose dandruff, prevents dryness."

Hair tonics had great names: Lucky Tiger, Wildroot Crème Oil, Kreml, Pinol, Athenian, Ambree Lavender Water, Hungarian Essence. And, of course, Sur-Lay.

Some tonics would go on to become favorite home brands. Wildroot became famous for its slogan "Get Wildroot Crème Oil, Charlie."

And some would remain trade brands. Lucky Tiger, a great World War I flying ace of a name, was a staple of barbershops all over.

Picking your favorite hair tonic was one thing, but applying it was an art unto itself. I watched many a greaser practice this art in the fifties at the juvenile delinquent junior high I attended. Here the social order was controlled not by the popular kids, but by the primates, the big kids—it was survival of the fittest.

Many a lunch period found me huddled in the bathroom, trying to avoid the likes of Russell "Little Man" Combs, the undisputed thug king of Ross N. Robinson Junior High School (R.N.R.J.H.S.). He was a benevolent dictator, if you gave up your lunch money peacefully. And he was a greaser king with a pompadour that touched God.

Russell was the quarterback for one year (he was too old to play by the time he reached eighth grade and by ninth grade he had enlisted). And I still don't know how he got his football helmet on over that sweeping mound of hair.

But he had the damnedest hair you've ever seen.

I would watch Russell anoint his hair in the bathroom, or sometimes in the locker room, I was fortunate enough to have him in my gym class, giving him the opportunity to terrorize me twice a day.

He used Wildroot Crème Oil in the flask-sized bottle. The operative word in the name was oil and that's what Russell wanted. That's what we all wanted with our hair in the fifties: hair with sheen.

Russell would position himself in front of the mirror, his feet shoulder-width apart. Then he would scrunch down. He didn't have to scrunch down to see himself in the mirror. Russell was not tall. His position at the top of the pecking order came from the fact that he was strong, he was old (he must have been held back at least twice), and he was mean as a black snake. And he was fearless when it came to lunchtime fighting. I'd seen him take on guys half a head taller and make them cry.

He would literally dump half the bottle in his cupped left hand, then bring it together with his right, rub briskly, and then massage the ointment into his hair, always progressing in a backward motion. Once he had his hair drenched in oil, he casually flicked his comb from the back right pocket.

Russell carried a metal comb that gleamed in the fluorescent glow of the boy's bathroom. He would cup his left hand over the frontispiece of his mane masterpiece while he eased the comb back through the wings on the side. He had a slight wave in his hair that he liked to show off and he made sure that every hair was heading straight backward, exactly parallel to the ground. Then, without moving his left hand from its position guarding the pump of hair on the top, he would reach across and comb the other wing back, too, finishing with a flourish. He used three strokes on the crown, one up and in the center, and then blended strokes on the side to make sure that it was all of a piece.

Finally Russell would step back from the mirror, still in his spread stance, and admire the beauty of it all. And then, as he flipped the comb back in the pocket, he would wink. The wink said it all: perfecto!

The purpose of the ubiquitous hair tonics wasn't entirely for male pulchritude, or so their manufacturers claimed. Barber-college textbook-writer Sherman Trusty divided hair tonics into two categories:

"Straight tonics," he claimed, were intended "to correct such conditions as dandruff, dryness, oiliness and itching. They have medicinal properties."

Hairdressing preparations, which he defined as "oil mixtures and hair creams containing various proportions of lanolin and mineral oils," were "intended only to add glossiness and hold the hair in place."

Trusty identified fourteen "specific purposes" of hair tonics, including "to stop itching of the scalp, to stimulate circulation, to help prevent dandruff, to provide a pleas-

ant perfume, to make the hair lie down, to help check an
over-perspiring scalp and to add a lifelike resemblance to
the hair."

With hair tonic having so many purposes, the Sur-Lay
folks, and the Lucky Tiger folks, and the Wildroot Crème
Oil folks, and the Vitalis folks must have thought they'd
stumbled onto a gold mine. You couldn't find a family
that didn't have a bottle of hair tonic tucked away somewhere in the lavatory.

And for a time these manufacturers did have the keys
to the vault.

Marsha McNeer, a retired Atlanta advertising execu-
tive, remembers walking past the barbershop on a Saturday afternoon in the fifties and nearly being overcome by
the aroma of Lucky Tiger wafting out. "The boys that got
Lucky Tiger would be fighting the flies off their hair the
rest of the day."

By the fifties Lucky Tiger had had a long history already, none of it particularly good.

In 1927 the American Medical Association labeled
Lucky Tiger a "dangerous nostrum sold for dandruff,
exzema and sore feet." At the time Tiger was making a
number of claims for its tonic, including, "kills dandruff
germs—stops itching. Corrects exzematous conditions of
the scalp, promotes luxuriant growth . . . stops falling
hair . . . (cures) chigger, mosquito and other insect bites."

An accompanying pamphlet claimed it was even good for "tired, aching and sore feet."

The AMA sent a bottle to its lab and discovered that in addition to alcohol Lucky Tiger contained sodium salicylate and sodium arsenite. Sodium salicylate is one of the ingredients in Doan's backache pills. Sodium arsenite is a carcinogen, a banned pesticide, and a form of arsenic, which led the *Handbook of Buying* from Consumers' Research to put Lucky Tiger on its Not Recommended list in 1931. Four years later the company dropped sodium arsenite from its formula.

In 1941 Lucky Tiger was back in trouble with the Federal Trade Commission because of its claim that it would "remove the cause of dandruff." The company agreed to stop advertising that the tonic "had any therapeutic value in treating" dandruff and also agreed to stop promising that Lucky Tiger would "stop itching, prevent loss of hair or eliminate scalp disorders."

Left to fend for itself as a mere tonic, sales went into a steep decline. In 1958 the company decided to make a last ditch effort to move up into the big leagues of home hair tonic brands, alongside Wildroot Crème Oil, Brylcreem ("a little dab will do ya"), and Vitalis. The company engaged a "motivational researcher" who recommended new packaging (lose the lady and the tiger, insert a cartoon tiger) and a rock music theme in its ads.

The company started the new campaign in 1958, touting "Improved Lucky Tiger Hair Tonic with LT-6 is the complete all-purpose hair preparation, Superior for grooming, Prevention of Dryness, Control of Loose Dandruff and Stimulation of the Scalp." LT-6 was one of those stealth secret ingredients that everybody loved in the fifties (we didn't want the Russians knowing what was in our hair tonics). LT-6 was actually oxyquinoline phosphate, an antiseptic and deodorizer. The new packaging and ad campaign seemed to work. By 1961 *Consumer Bulletin* was reporting that Lucky Tiger sales had tripled in just three years.

But then something happened. Have I mentioned these words before? The Beatles.

With the four lads came the Dry Look ("The Wethead is dead!" commercials shouted) and gone were the hair tonics. Hippie hair was supposed to flow with the breeze; it was a part of the personal philosophy of the wearer.

Even when the Wethead returned in the eighties, with NBA coach Pat Riley and *Wall Street* movie character Gordon Gekko, hair tonics didn't. They were replaced with modern up-to-date hairstyling products like mousses and gels.

Hair tonic has never been the same since the fifties. Not even Sur-Lay.

Chapter 7

Tools of the Trade

While I was traveling around researching this book, I visited my old college chum Chris Wohlwend. I found him reared back in his chair, watching a tape of Robert Altman's *Nashville* on the TV. He looked relaxed enough to fall asleep in his reclining TV chair. But Wohlwend isn't lounging in a La-Z-Boy—the recliner in his living room is a barber chair.

"I don't think there's any doubt that the recliner people took their idea from the barbershop," he says. "Look at the similarities: headrest, foot support, reclining capability. All you need to ask is which came first. And everybody knows which came first: the barber chair."

The barber chair was the original La-Z-Boy, the original chaise lounge, the original recliner.

Barbers were cranking their customers back and raising their customers' feet long before those Michigan farm boys Edwin Shoemaker and his cousin Edward Knabusch invented the reclining chair in 1928. (The two Eds didn't add a footrest to their La-Z-Boy recliner until the fifties.)

As long as there have been barbers, there have been

barber chairs. Barber chairs in engravings from the Civil War era share many features with modern chairs: they sat high and featured upholstered backs and a footrest, albeit a detached footrest. The backs didn't recline so the patron's head did instead; when it came time for a shave, the customer would just lean his head back. To adjust for customers of varying heights the barber had a low, wide box to stand on. (You don't want a man with a razor in his hand standing over you on a wobbly footstool.)

The first-factory manufactured chairs date to about 1850.

The first one-piece reclining barber chair with an attached footrest was patented in 1878 by the Archer Company of Saint Louis. Archer quickly followed it with a chair that raised and lowered mechanically. Eugene Berninghaus of Cincinnati improved on Archer's design with the first reclining *and* revolving chair, the Paragon, which allowed the barber to "command the advantage of light."

The chair manufacturer who learned from the others was Theodore Koch of Chicago. Koch incorporated all these innovations into his chairs and quickly became *the* name in barber chairs. He sold more than 35,000 chairs in the period before 1885.

Then, in 1900, a German immigrant named Ernest Koken devised a hydraulic-operated chair. Check the footrest of your current barber's chair—there's a good chance it reads Koken. He also patented the "joystick" side lever, which allowed a barber to control all the mechanical functions of the chair in one convenient lever.

Koken's innovations in the barber chair soon made him the industry standard. Most of Koken's chairs—and most barber chairs of the nineteenth century—were made of oak or maple. It wasn't until after World War I that the porcelain-enameled iron chair became popular.

Barber chairs really came of age in the period after World War I. They became monstrous thrones, often weighing three hundred pounds or more, with elaborate chrome and enamel designs. When I was a kid and climbed up into that giant chair, I felt swallowed up. I just assumed that the chair was bolted to the floor. In fact I thought there was some giant mechanism in the base-ment, a hydraulic system that enabled the chair to go up and down with ease. It turns out it was the weight of the chair that held it firm. That round pedestal base hid noth-ing except a few squares of asphalt tile. But the base itself was usually filled with oil-soaked sand.

Barber and barbershop historian Frank Chirco of Cal-ifornia says the chairs made in the middle years of the twentieth century were so good they were, well, too good. "The barber chair companies made chairs that lasted for-ever. Put them out of business. The chairs were so good there was no reason to replace them."

Chirco says his personal barber chair was manufac-tured in 1953. "It's all leather, simple hydraulic, cast iron. If you take halfway decent care, they're fine."

My barber Wib's chairs date from 1935. "They suppos-edly cost $1,200, which was a lot of money back then. I think my dad bought a house in the forties and only paid

$1,700 for it. A fellow tried to buy one off me just yesterday. I told him I had four kids and I'd promised each one of them a chair when I retire."

As early as 1911 barber college instructor A. B. Moler was advising prospective barbers to take care in purchasing a chair. "Among the higher grade chairs the hydraulic chair that raises and lowers by a lever arrangement is the most desirable. A chair of this kind should be upholstered in leather or something similar so that it can be easily cleaned. . . . Select a pedestal base chair as the sprawling legs are always in the way of your feet."

Sherman Trusty thought the chair was so important to the barber that in his 1958 textbook, *The Art and Science of Barbering,* he called it "the home base of the barber's income. Around it is the area of his performances."

Trusty noted a phenomenon that is still true today: "Barbers become sentimentally attached to a particular chair."

If you don't believe that try buying your barber's chair off him.

The sun is just peering over the horizon as the yawning merchant unlocks his door. He sheds his straw hat and suit coat, dons a white smock, and heads back outside, a heavy key in hand. He inserts the key in the base of his sign and begins cranking. The spring-driven motor accepts its wind and soon the candy-striped pole is spinning. The stripes begin at the top and sprint quickly to the bottom of the pole, only to reappear magically at the top for a return trip. Little boys will spend many hours peering up at this magic stick.

The barber pole is the barber's beacon, perhaps the best-known symbol in the world, better known than the pharmacist's mortar and pestle, the pawnbroker's three gold balls, and the optometrist's oversized eyeglasses.

That's a scene from the turn of the century—the previous turn of the century.

Barbers don't wind their poles anymore. Barber poles are all electric-powered now. But the message is the same as it was a hundred years ago when early rising barbers arrived in their shops, ready to shave the town's elite. The red, white, and blue candy-cane pole is a siren to the shaggy and the scruffy: come inside, it cries, have thy hair clipped and thy beard trimmed.

But it makes no sense. Why would a party-trimmed staff represent the barber's trade?

It's a long story, worthy even of a chapter.

Let's begin with an account of the origin of the barber pole by the man whose name is now synonymous with barber pole, Bill Marvy of Saint Paul, Minnesota. Fully half of all barbershops today have Marvy-manufactured poles out front. Marvy is dead (since 1993 at age eighty-four) but in 1981 he told the *Chicago Tribune,* "The barber pole goes back to the barber/surgeon of the Middle Ages. In addition to cutting hair, he'd pull teeth, let blood, use leeches, lance boils. The barber would hang red and white bandages out, symbols of his work, and they'd blow in the wind and twist around. The red and white stripes represent blood and the linen. Around the turn of the century, they started using red, white, and blue stripes—patriotic."

The barber pole question is indeed a popular one, puzzled over for at least three centuries. A reader of *British Apollo*, a magazine published in London, wrote in 1708: "Why a barber at port-hole Puts forth a party-coloured pole?"

The answer, in verse:

In ancient Rome, when men lov'd fighting,
And wounds and scars took much delight in,
Man-menders then had noble pay,
Which we call surgeons to this day.
'Twas orderd that a hughe long pole,
With bason deck'd should grace the hole,
To guide the wounded, who unlopt
Could walk, on stumps the others hopt
But, when they ended all their wars,
And men grew out of love with scars,
Their trade decaying; to keep swimming
They joyn'd the other trade of trimming,
And on their poles to publish either,
Thus twisted both their trades together.

One of the earliest references to the barber pole is found in *The Athenian Oracle*, published in 1334. "The

barber's art was so beneficial to the publick, that he who
first brought it up in Rome had, as authors relate, a statue
erected to his memory. In England they were in some
sort the surgeons of old times, into whose art those beautiful leeches, our fair virgins, were also accustomed to be
initiated. In cities and corporate towns they still retain
their name Barber-Chirurgions. They therefore used to
hang their basons out upon poles to make known at distance to the weary and wounded traveler where all might
have recourse. They use poles, as some inns still gibbet
their signs, across a town."

There is a picture of the pole in *Comenii Orbis Sensualium Pictus (The Visible World)*, the first illustrated
schoolbook, which was published in 1658. The drawing
shows the interior of a barbershop where a customer is
being bled by the barber. In his hand the customer holds
a staff with a bandage twisted around it.

When the practices of the barber and the surgeon
were legally separated in the early 1700s, the British
House of Peers entertained (but did not pass) a bill that
would have required barbers and surgeons to have different styles of poles. The barber pole was to be blue and
white striped, with no appendages; the surgeon's pole
would be the same but with a galley pot and a red rag.

The Antiquarian Repertory, published in the early
1800s, tells the tale this way. "The barber's pole has been
the subject of many conjectures, some conceiving it to
have originated from the word poll or head, with several
other conceits far-fetched and as unmeaning; but the true

intention of the party coloured staff was to show that the master of the shop practised surgery and could breathe a vein as well a mow a beard: such a staff being to this day by every village practitioner put in the hand of the patient undergoing the operation of phlebotomy. The white band, which encompasses the staff, was meant to represent the fillet thus elegantly twined about it."

Tonsorial professor Sherman Trusty tells another variation in his 1958 textbook. "The most reliable story is that the pole originated when bloodletting was the most typical service of the barber. The two spiral ribbons painted around the pole were symbolic of the two bandages used in bloodletting. One ribbon represented the bandage bound around the arm before the surgery was performed, and the other one afterwards. The true colors of the barber emblem are white and red. Red, white, and blue are widely used in America. This is due partly to the fact that the national flag has these colors. But red and white are regarded by most authorities as the true colors of the barber pole. Another interpretation of the colors of the barber pole is that red was symbolic of blood, blue of the veins, and white of the bandage."

Whatever the origin—and most agree it comes from the bloody rags of the barber-surgeon—A. B. Moler has it right in his 1911 textbook: "As the barber pole is the advertisement for the place, it should be a worthy representative."

Enter William Marvy, who fashioned the most worthy representative.

Marvy, a Minnesota wholesaler who sold barber supplies on his own out of the trunk of his car, was a visionary. Other barber supply salesmen looked at barber poles and saw a limited market (how often would a barber need a new pole?); Marvy saw opportunity. He saw rotting wooden shafts, rusting metal bodies, decaying plastic gears. He saw poles shattered by vandals and battered by weather.

So on New Year's Day in 1950 he sat on the floor in his basement and drew up the plans for a new kind of barber pole. It wouldn't rust because it would be made of aluminum and the motor wouldn't seize up because it would use stainless steel castings. The striped pole wouldn't rot because it would be made of plastic; and it wouldn't break because it would be covered by a shatterproof Lucite shell. And an electric motor would mean no more cranking.

On that day a half century ago William Marvy invented a better barber pole. And then he wrote up a sales brochure to match: "More pulling power than the Pied Piper. . . . Draws customers like honey bees. . . . As modern as a jet plane; ruggedly built as a bank vault."

He took his "Six Ways Better" pole to the barber supply trade show in Chicago's Palmer House that summer and amazed everyone in attendance. *The Wall Street Journal* called the Marvy pole the first real improvement in the barber pole in a quarter of a century.

Barbers stood in line just to get on the waiting list to buy a Marvy pole. By 1956 he had sold more than five thousand. When he began making the Marvy pole in 1950 there were five other barber-pole makers in the country: two in Chicago, one in Saint Louis, one in Los Angeles, and one in Winston-Salem, North Carolina. Soon there was only one.

At its peak in 1967 Marvy's factory in Saint Paul was running two shifts a day of twelve to fifteen men each. That was the year Marvy manufactured its fifty-thousandth pole. Marvy estimated at the time that half of all barbershops had a Marvy pole.

That was the high watermark for barber poles. Pretty soon just about every barber had one. But a quarter century later, in 1991, barber-pole sales had plummeted to a record low of 487.

Where another barber supply salesman might see saturation, Marvy saw potential. Next he devised a pole for unisex salons with the words "Hair Stylist" on a stripe. He invented a pole for dog grooming salons with leaping pink poodles on a stripe. He even devised a gambling pole with green and yellow stripes for an Atlantic City casino. (That idea hasn't caught on too well yet.)

And he went back to his roots, adding barber supplies to his lines: Mar-V-Cide disinfectant, Marvy combs, Marvy brushes, Marvy scissors, even Marvy Afro clips.

In 1982 William Marvy was elected to the Barber Hall of Fame, the only nonbarber among the Hall's thirty-three members. The Hall's electors said he had truly changed an industry, breathing life into an aspect of the business that constituted the only advertising most barbers ever did.

In his almost half century in the barber-pole business William Marvy sold his poles to the White House and to the Navy and to Las Vegas casinos. But his favorite sale was to a northern Minnesota ice fisherman who wanted it as a beacon, to help him find his way back to his cabin at night. The man returned his Marvy barber pole a week later; said it didn't work. After close questioning it came out that it didn't work for what he wanted it for. It seemed too many people were lining up at his door wanting haircuts.

There's more to a barbershop than a barber chair and a barber pole. But the other tools—clippers, combs, razors, tonics, and lotions—are relatively low-priced in comparison to a pole (five hundred dollars) and a chair, which can cost upward of four thousand dollars (the Koken Sir with a motorized headrest).

Even with a four-grand outlay for a chair, barbering is still one of the cheapest professions to enter.

In 1911 Moler touted the low capital expenditure necessary to ply one's trade. "One of the desirable features about learning this trade is that you may at any time conduct a place of your own with little capital and without risk. Most men desire sometime in the future to be their own boss, if not at present, and in choosing this business as a livelihood, a business of your own is within your reach. A place may be established with little expense and still be neat in arrangement or it may be equipped as elaborately as desired."

Moler was an early practitioner of feng shui, even if he had never heard the term. "The general arrangement (of the barber shop) should be in harmony. In purchasing any equipment try and collect articles of furniture that will harmonize and each will add to the appearance of the other. Look to the trimmings and try and have the general tone of your place carried out in each article. Do not have an expensive mirror case and cheap surroundings and most important of all look to the sanitary feature. The latest designed mirror case among the most expensive varieties at present are those with the washstand made a part of the cabinet. This supplies hot and cold running water immediately in front of the barber and saves many steps during the day's work."

Feng shui may sway customers but for Moler money talked: "It has also been demonstrated that with the shampoo apparatus directly in front of the customer a third more shampoos will be had by the customer than the style that requires the customer and barber to leave the chair and go to the washstand for the rinsing. . . . A vibrator for face and scalp massage brings in splendid revenue and should be a part of the equipment. . . . If cigars, tobacco and toilet articles are handled, a display case and wall case is necessary. A neatly arranged display of toilet preparations not only adds to the appearance of the shop, but affords an income not to be overlooked."

So what does a barber need? What are the tools of the trade? They aren't much different today than they were sixty-six years ago when the Journeymen Barbers Union listed them in its textbook under the heading "Instruments and Accessories Used in the Practice of Barbering":

Strop
Hone
Razor
Shears
Hair Clippers
Comodone Extractor
Tweezer Needle
Styptic Powder
Combs
Brushes
Hair Duster
Soaps
Jacket

(About the jacket Moler cautioned, "No barber should work at the chair without a jacket, as it looks unprofessional and untidy to see a barber at a chair in his shirtsleeves or wearing the old style apron.")

There are tools of the trade and then there are tools of the trade.

But the greatest of these is the comb.

Sherman Trusty even formulated what we might call the Four Commandments of the Comb:

1. That the teeth be shaped so that they feed into and through the hair—well pointed, not too wide nor thick; of the proper length, and the right distance apart.
2. That the teeth not be sharp, but tapered, rounded.
3. That it be flexible, capable of being bent to take the nape of the head without breaking.
4. That its size be commensurate with the particular use to which it is put: fine comb for edge and detail; coarse comb for roughing in.

When it comes to combs, Moler also has some apt advice. "In the selection of combs, the handmade horn comb is preferable. It should be a tapering comb of medium size, and one that can be well handled in long or short hair. Aluminum combs are considered by some the most sanitary, but there is an objection to this style of comb, as the teeth often come in contact with the blade of your shears."

Not good. Especially with electric shears—buzzzzz!

He continues, "Among the cheaper grades are the 'machine made' horn combs, which are usually more blunt and less convenient. The heavy rubber combs are of no service to the barber on account of their thickness. Celluloid combs are of no value, for in singeing hair they are liable to catch fire." Also not good, a burning comb. Moler continued, "Great care should be taken to keep a comb perfectly clean. Thread or string is very handy in cleaning it. Take a half dozen or dozen threads fastened at both ends and comb through them until teeth are thoroughly cleaned."

Would that Trusty were alive today he could go on late-night TV hawking his Hair Combing System, teaching drowsy viewers Trusty's Hair Management System:

"Grasping the comb. Hold with the fingers and palm so that the tip of the first finger falls about at the division between the fine and coarse teeth, and the cushion tip of the thumb on the back just below the first finger; the other three fingers are bent over the part enclosed in such a way that the balls of these fingers aid in holding the comb firmly. It will be found that finger one is scarcely bent or curved. Hold the comb firmly but not tightly. Holding the comb thus will facilitate comb management."

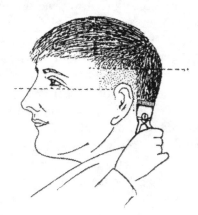

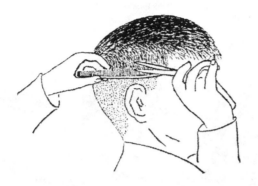

Trusty actually goes on for a mind-numbing nine more paragraphs concluding with his seminal section on "Parallel structure in shear-and-comb work." He tells barbers, "Generally the shears and comb are held parallel to each other, but not when it is awkward to do so, as when doing the sideburns and the mastoid regions."

So you see: barbers take their combs very, very seriously.

Chapter 8

A Close Shave

The shave is so closely associated with the haircut—you know, shave and a haircut, two bits—that it is jarring to discover how few barbers still offer shaves. It's not that they don't know how; shaving is still part of the barber college curriculum. It's that there's no demand. And even when there is, it's an unprofitable sideline.

I found a newspaper clipping about a barber in south Florida who still prided himself on his shave. So I headed the car south to Big Bob's in Fort Lauderdale.

Shaving is an art, proclaimed A. B. Moler in the very first barbers' manual, the aptly titled *The Barbers' Manual*, published in 1911.

"Shaving is an art," agreed barber Bob, who had me reclined in chair number one, in the front corner of his shop. Today he is preparing to give me, literally, the shave of my life. And I am hoping like heck that Bob is an artist, since he has a razor sharp enough to cut cubic zirconium at my very vulnerable throat.

Big Bob's is located in a strip mall off the beaten path, where, judging from the other clientele, blond hair comes to dye. But dyeing is not the specialty of the house. Nor is shaving; I had to make a special appointment with Big Bob. Big Bob's is just a barbershop that happens to be owned by a shaving master.

Big Bob begins with two hot towel treatments to make sure my beard is soft and my pores are open before touching the razor to my cheek. As you might expect, Big Bob has big hands but they are gentle with the razor.

Bob gently massages warm shaving lather into my skin while he surveys my beard. He isn't looking for a starting point; that was fixed in his mind three decades ago when he learned to shave. He is checking for hazards: facial imperfections, zits, a protruding Adam's apple.

The secret is the foam, warm and rich, he says. "You must use good soap." Just the feel, so much more soothing than the canned foam I spread across my face, is enough to settle me deeper into the chair. There is no mess as he lathers my beard. He is smooth and experienced. The soap tickles the ridge of my ear, curls just onto my lip, then settles like a mask across my face.

I've seen countless gangsters and cowboys succumb to the pleasures of a barber's shave in movies, but this is my first professional shave. And not my last.

Bob drapes a hot towel over the foam, curling the ends of the cloth over my eyes, leaving only a gap for my nose.

He removes the towel and lathers my face again, this time more deliberately.

As the foam and my face become one, Bob reaches for his razor, a long blade of the kind favored in films by villains. His is honed to an even sharpness. He runs it over his fingernail because the nail picks up any place on the blade that isn't even.

He starts tentatively at my right sideburn, but once he gets going the strokes are swift and strong: one, two, three. He uses short strokes, not big flourishes. My right temple is smooth and tingly. Four, five, six . . . fourteen strokes later and my cheek is as smooth as a cue ball. Only a hint of shaving foam remains at the base of my earlobes.

After sweeping away all my whiskers, he lathers his hands again and again rubs shaving cream on my face. He rubs his razor on a sharpening stone and returns to shave me again, this time against the grain. "I don't always go

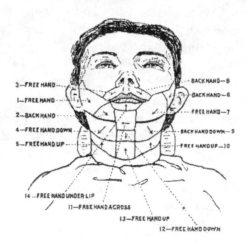

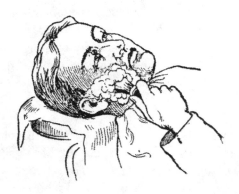

against the grain. It depends on how sensitive the skin is."
Bob has the hands of a surgeon, swift and sure, which is exactly what you want when a man has a razor at your throat.

In minutes the foam, and my beard, is gone. Bob is an
artist with his razor; he doesn't even nick me.

Then he reaches to the back bar for a flask of skin
bracer that he says is antiseptic. He rubs it gently over my
face. It is antiseptic all right; it stings like hell but his gentle fanning soothes the burn. My pores seem to constrict
and then open up. It's a feeling I've never had.

Next he kneads a fragrant aftershave into my face, using a towel to fan. It's a familiar smell. "That's where the
old barbershop got its smell, when the barber would fan
the aftershave out into the place."

When I touch my face it is like I'm touching someone
else's face. It reminds me of my first shave in eighth grade,
when my father ran his electric razor over my upper lip. I
kept touching it because it felt so different. My shave was

as smooth as the marble curbstone outside. "I've never had a closer shave," I told him as I left. My shave was so close I didn't have to shave again for two days.

I walked out feeling like a million bucks. And smelling that way, too. Quite a bargain for ten bucks.

Women take mud baths, get their faces massaged, their legs waxed, and their nails manicured. Men get, uh, haircuts. The closest guy thing to all these pampered-woman experiences is an old-fashioned barbershop shave.

You just sit back and let the barber do what Mr. King Gillette's greatest—and only—invention normally does: whisk that unsightly facial hair away.

Not very many barbers do shaves anymore. Not that they can't. Most every barber board in America requires barber college graduates to pass a shaving test before he or she can get a license. It's just that there's not much call for it. So barbers don't even know how much to charge. In my travels around the country for this book, I found that about one in ten offers shaves and even they don't know how much to charge anymore (I got prices ranging from five dollars to twenty dollars). So you have to hunt if you want a barbershop shave. But it's worth the hunt.

It is perhaps the most sublime experience an adult male can have, and yet, because of changing fashions, it is rarely experienced.

How do barbers learn to shave so close and yet so smooth? By shaving foam off balloons in barber college, I was told time and again. But even as I heard the legend, I couldn't find anyone who actually learned on balloons. Most cultivated the art on men of the street.

Jerry Biggerstaff, a barber in Marion, North Carolina, says at his barber college, "That meant winos. Once in barber college I finished shaving this wino and he came around to the mirror and was admiring his face. He says, 'That's a good shave, that's a good shave.' And then he grabbed the witch hazel and started drinking it before I could grab it out of his hand!"

The Textbook of Practical and Scientific Barbering, published in 1947, trains the budding barber in what Ohio barber Ed Jeffers calls "the classic fourteen-stroke shave," beginning with a steam towel. Once the towel is removed the barber is ready to apply the lather. And lathering for a professional shave is not just squirting a gob of Barbasol in your hand and rubbing it in *The Textbook* teaches.

When it's time to shave, the artful barber doesn't just grab up the razor and whisk it across your face. Like bunting in baseball, there is a right way and a wrong way to grip. *The Textbook* says, "The razor is placed firmly in the hand but not too rigid as this will set the wrist muscles, thus interfering with a free movement."

Sherman Trusty in *The Art and Science of Barbering* compares the actual deployment of the razor to cutting bread. "There is a clean cut analogy between slicing a loaf of bread and shaving. A loaf of bread is not sliced by

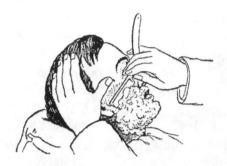

pushing a knife straight through it; a sawing, sliding stroke is used, with practically no pressure applied. This illustrates the fundamental principle of shaving."

Now the barber is ready to shave, beginning with stroke one, the right cheek. Four strokes later the right half of the face is completed and the barber is instructed to sharpen his razor on the leather strop. He then moves to the right side of the customer and stroke six. "With the back hand stroke, shave the center and half of the left side of the upper lip. With stroke eleven the barber finishes shaving the chin whiskers and moves to the Adam's apple area. The final stroke, stroke fourteen on the lower lip, winds it up."

Then the barber is instructed to do it all again, this time without lather, using only water.

I'm glad I didn't know all this before I got my first barber shave. I would have been so attentive to technique I would have forgotten to relax and enjoy it.

And I did enjoy it.

Shaving goes back a long, long way . . . to Alexander the Great if you believe the history books. Alexander, or Great, as his friends called him, ordered the soldiers in his Macedonian army to shave before going into battle, according to most every writer who has ever addressed the subject. Sherman Trusty, in *The Art and Science of Barbering*, says, "Alexander the Great . . . commanded all his soldiers to be clean-shaven. This command was given after losing several battles with the Persians who caught his soldiers, the Macedonians, by the beard and threw them to the ground and slaughtered them." William Andrews, in *At the Sign of the Barber's Pole: Studies in Hirsute History*, concurs with this reading of history. "The Macedonian soldiers were ordered by Alexander to shave, lest their beards should be handles for the enemy to capture them by."

California barber and professional barber-history cynic Frank Chirco says Trusty isn't trustworthy and Andrews's assertion is doubtful. "First, Alexander the Great didn't have authority to do that. Second: think about it—you've got a sword in one hand and a shield in the other.

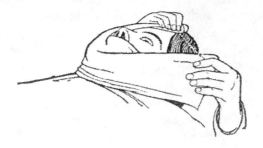

What are you grabbing with? You'd have to put down one to grab your opponent's beard. Which one do you put down? The truth is Alexander was very young and didn't have a beard. So his men shaved in imitation of Alexander." So Alexander did more than conquer Persia; he also conquered the Persian custom of shaving.

Alexander was overcoming a lot of history when he popularized the custom of shaving. Beards were as old as time and were considered a symbol of manhood, of strength and wisdom and dignity. Most of the Greek gods were bearded: check out a painting of Zeus on his throne, looking like the star of the touring company of *Hair*. Or Atlas, already carrying the weight of the world, and forced by fashion to carry an extra couple of pounds of facial hair. Moses had a magnificent beard, so magnificent that full beards are often called Mosaic beards.

It wasn't that nobody shaved before Alexander. Moses commanded his people to shave because of a plague. And Joseph shaved when ordered to appear before the pharaoh. But it wasn't until Alexander that the smooth look caught on. Even then it was only for a time. Since Alex's time shaving has come in and out and in and out of fashion. And usually for no rhyme or reason save the masses were following the lead of a popular ruler or military general or rock star. When wisdom is king, people grow beards. And when the youth culture is king, people shave.

Early in his reign the Roman emperor Hadrian (A.D. 76–138) grew a beard to cover unsightly warts and scars. Suddenly all his subjects, even the ones who didn't have warts or scars, began growing beards. Hadrian's beard became so popular—and so famous—that a succession of Roman emperors adopted the style.

Andrews, in *At the Sign of the Barber's Pole*, tells the story of an English king who grew a beard because he didn't trust his barber. "The barber of an English king boasted, says a story, that he must be the most loyal man in the realm, as he had every day the regal throat at his mercy. The king was startled at the observation, and concluded that the barbarous idea could never have entered an honest head, and for the future he resolved to grow a beard as a precautionary measure against summary execution."

Pope Julius II (1503–1513) was famous for three things: bribing his way into the papacy; cajoling Michelangelo into painting the ceiling of the Sistine Chapel (for which Julius would eventually be punished by having Rex Harrison portray him in the movie); and becoming the first pope to let his beard grow. He sprouted whiskers, he said, "in order to inspire the greater respect among the faithful."

There has always been a bit of hostility between the shaven and the unshaven. Andrews tells the story of the Eastern potentate visited by a clean-shaven British ambassador. "The Eastern monarch flew into a passion when the beardless visitor was presented. 'Had my master measured wisdom by the beard,' came the ready retort, 'he would have sent a goat.'"

The clean-shaven look of Julius II didn't last long. The beard was revived a few years later by British monarch King Henry VIII (who reigned 1509–1547). Andrews notes

---

Shave and a Haircut, Two Bits

Claude Russell's price list is simple. It's posted on the mirror of his Tennessee barbershop: $13 HAIRCUTS 50 PERCENT OFF.

That's his way of telling customers his price. "Ken and I decided to go up to $6.50 in January." Ken is his brother. They usually raise their rates in concert but it isn't price fixing because they don't agree on everything. "Ken, he gets ten dollars for a Flattop."

You can get a pretty good haircut for ten dollars or less in America. Sometimes you can even get a really good haircut.

My barber Wib told me a story about his price. "This fellow come in, looked at my sign (HAIRCUTS $9.50) and said, 'I can go over to Indiana and get one for five dollars.' I said, 'Oh, I can give you a five-dollar haircut if that's what you want.'"

The last time you could get a shave and a haircut for "two bits" (a quarter) was in 1931. Adjusting for inflation that would be about $2.50 today. And I don't know anywhere you can get a shave and a haircut for $2.50 today. It's seven bucks and up just about everywhere.

Even if you pay ten bucks to your barber, it's a bargain. Where else can you get an hour's worth of entertainment—and a haircut—that cheap?

---

not everyone was in favor of the new fashion. "The authorities at Lincoln's Inn prohibited lawyers wearing beards from sitting at the great table, unless they paid double commons; but it is highly probable that this was before 1535, when the king ordered his courtiers to 'poll their hair, and permit the crisp beard to grow.'"

In the 1950s Burma-Shave made light of Henry VIII's unruly whiskers and wives with this roadside doggerel:

Henry the Eighth
Sure had trouble
Short-term wives
Long-term stubble.

Edward VI, Henry's only son, tried to reverse the beard trend with, what else, a tax. Andrews writes, "The amount was graduated according to the condition of the person wearing this hirsute adornment. An entry has often been reproduced from the Burghmote Book of Canterbury, made in the second year of the reign of Edward VI, to the effect that the Sheriff of Canterbury and another paid their dues for wearing beards, 3s. 4d. and 1s 8d." That would be about $2.25 in today's money.

Edward's sister, Elizabeth, tried to one-up him by increasing the beard tax. Parliament put the price at three shilling, four pence for "every beard of above a fortnight's growth." The law was a disaster, never enforced, even mocked.

That's a small price compared to the Russian beard tax.

"Peter the Great was wishful that his subjects should conform to the prevailing fashion," Andrews writes. "In 1705 he imposed a tax upon all those who wore either a beard or a moustache, varying from thirty to one hundred roubles per annum. It was fixed according to the rank of the taxpayer. A peasant, for instance, was only required to pay two dengops, equal to one copeck, whenever he passed through the gate of a town. This tax gave rise to much discontent, and in enforcing it the utmost vigilance had to be exercised to prevent an outbreak in the country."

The law was extended to Saint Petersburg, which had previously been exempt, in 1714. If you couldn't pay? Then it was off to the labor camps. When Peter died, his successor Catherine I confirmed all the beard taxes.

Peter II also disliked facial hair but did relent and permit peasants working in agriculture to wear beards. Empress Anne hated hairy faces more than the two Peters and in 1731 required that all other woolly workers would pay double the amount of all taxes in addition to the beard tax. Russia quickly became very clean-shaven. It was not until the ascension of Catherine II in 1762 that this anti-hairy hysteria abated. She immediately rescinded all beard taxes.

Later on in our own country Revolutionary War soldiers were as clean-shaven as Johnny Tremain (and their leader, the smooth-faced George Washington); Civil War soldiers were hairy; World War I doughboys were mustachioed; World War II soldiers were clean-shaven.

Lincoln was clean-shaven when he ran for president of

the United States, then grew a beard after a letter from a little girl who told him he looked goofy. (Actually eleven-year-old Grace Bedell of Westfield, New York, urged him to grow a beard because "you would look a great deal better for your face is so thin.")

Except for hippies and latter-day country music fans, beards were out of favor for most of the twentieth century.

With the new century it seems to be anything goes. Creative types favor close-cropped beards; baseball players go for those Vandyke things that cover only the chin and upper lip; basketball players shave everything, including the top of the head; and ZZ Top continues to hold on to the Rip Van Winkle look.

Chapter 9

Toupee for a Day

Call them what you will: Hairpieces. Toupees. Wigs. Rugs. Toups. *Shmatte* (that's Yiddish for rag).

They are still with us. Hair transplants and Rogaine and Propescia haven't wiped out the toupee industry. Don't believe me? Check out any senior citizen dance. There's usually three to five old guys with acrylic-looking hair.

Before the Hair Club of America and Apollo Hair Systems, barbers were the primary source for hairpieces.

In the early days, they even made their own.

William Andrews, in his 1904 book *At the Sign of the Barber's Pole: Studies in Hirsute History*, traces toupees all the way back to the ancient Egyptians, which is a pretty long way, considering that "ancient Egyptians" usually refers to the Egyptian culture that thrived from 3100 B.C. through the rule of Ramses III, the last great Egyptian pharaoh, whose reign ended in 1166 B.C.

Men have been wearing rugs for five millennia. Whew! If you think about all the progress made in those five thousand years and how bad toupees still look, you've got to wonder where we've been putting our toupee R&D resources.

The Assyrians, who invaded Egypt in 671 B.C., picked up the periwig habit from their vanquished foe, and Assyrian sculptures frequently feature wigs. According to Andrews, many ancient nations fancied hairpieces, including "Persians, Medes, Lydians, Carians, Greeks, and Romans." The Roman name for them, *calerus*, meant "round cap."

Wigs were used to cover baldness, yes, but they were also used as a fashion accessory to enhance a fellow's attractiveness to the opposite sex.

As you might expect, this didn't sit well with religious leaders. The Greek theologian Clement of Alexandria so despised hairpieces that he would tell his bewigged followers who knelt at the altar to receive the blessing that his benediction remained on the hairpiece and didn't pass through to the worshipper. Andrews says early leaders of the Catholic Church "denounced the wig as an invention of the Evil One." Saint Jerome considered it unworthy of Christianity. Church councils from Constantinople to the Provincial Council at Tours condemned artificial hair. Andrews notes, "The wig was not tolerated, even if worn as a joke. 'There is no joke in the matter,' said the enraged Saint Bernard. 'Who wears a wig commits a mortal sin.'"

Wigs were late catching on in England. The earliest entry for a wig in the Royal Privy Purse expenses is December 1529: "Twenty shillings for a perwyke for Sexton, the king's fool." If it was for the court jester, you know it was a bad toupee.

The first king to be represented on the Great Seal in a wig was Charles II, who ruled from 1630 to 1685. He adopted the wig fashion after some initial resistance, according to Andrews. "Dr. Doran assures us that the king did not bring the fashion to Whitehall. 'He forbade the members of the Universities to wear periwigs, smoke tobacco, or to read their sermons. The members did all three, and Charles soon found himself doing two.'"

Diarist Samuel Pepys (1633–1703), a great follower of fashion, wrestled with the wig question, even going so far as to ask his barber, Mr. Jervas, for advice. "I did try two or three borders and periwigs, meaning to wear one, and yet I have no stomach for it; but that the pains of keeping my hair clean is great. He trimmed me, and at last I parted, but my mind was almost altered from my first purpose, from the trouble which I foresee in wearing them also." He eventually bought one from a wig maker but relied on Jervas the barber to repair it.

Is there a worse toupee on display anywhere than that of William Shatner, formerly of *Star Trek?* Well, one— Burt Reynolds. A once esteemed actor, Reynolds made a series of bad choices in the eighties when it came to roles and to toupees. When Reynolds filed for bankruptcy in 1996, he suffered the embarrassment of having to list debts to two toupee companies, including a whopping $121,796.62 owed to Edward Katz Hair Design and a smaller amount to Apollo Hair Systems, Inc.

And now dear reader, having made snide comments about the Bad Toupee Society members of both the modern and ancient world, I have to admit that in my closet, atop a white Styrofoam head, sits a mousy-brown toupee that would scare any small child who happened inside my wardrobe.

In 1975 I was talked into purchasing a toupee. By my mother, of course, who agreed to reimburse me. If memory serves, it was ninety-four dollars, plus tax, fitting thrown in free, from a hair-design shop called Hair by Troy. (That would be about three hundred dollars today; still a cheap rug.) It was made of real human hair and looked nothing at all like that dead cat that country singer Hank Snow used to park on his head at the Grand Ole Opry.

It looked good. It still looks good, sitting on that Styrofoam pedestal. It's just that my hair is no longer that color or length. Times have changed and so has my hair and my hairstyle. I really would look like the desperate bachelor at the Arthur Murray studio if I were to don it today.

I wore it for one week, then placed it back on that plastic head. I only take it out now and again for an occasional practical joke. When my eighteen-year-old son was a small boy, I put it on once to tease him. He screamed and jumped out of his skin.

It was an educational experience, wearing a wig for a week.

For one thing, I found out who my friends were. People who knew me well would look at me and burst out laughing. People who didn't know me quite so well would stare intently and then ask, "Did you get new glasses?"

I also learned a lot about myself. A friend who was in on the wig thing told me that Carl Reiner says the only way you can wear a wig is if you treat it like a hat. That's certainly what NBC weatherman Willard Scott does. Some days he has it on, others he leaves it at home. He isn't trying to cover up, to hide anything.

And that was something I could never do. For me the toupee was a cover-up and nothing more. It had nothing to do with fashion or wardrobe ("Pink shirt today? Think I'll match it with that pink toupee"). I was simply trying to pretend I wasn't bald. And you can't do that. If you are bald, you are bald and no fancy piece of fabric and fluff can alter that, no matter how well it matches the hair that rims your bald spot.

I frankly don't know how Carl Reiner or Willard Scott do it. For me the toupee was an embarrassing accident waiting to happen. Even though it was taped securely to my head, I knew a hurricane gale was going to blow in and tear my hair off.

I knew I couldn't fool everyone—there were too many people who knew me as a baldie—so I would be living a lie. I knew I would look, as humor columnist Dave Barry once said, like "an egg in the clutches of a giant spider."

To survive with a toupee, I would have to move away, start a whole new life, live like a Russian spy.

Certainly there are good toupees. Bruce Willis seems to have a closet full of them. But then Bruce Willis gets paid $20 million per movie, considerably more than my

standard book fee. And Willis wears them like a hat:
Crew cut for action role, long hair for villain, neat trim for
romantic lead. Occasionally he even goes natural.

Bob Kelly, a Manhattan toupee maker, told Gannett
News Service, "When somebody comes up to you and
says, 'Nice-looking toupee,' that means it's obvious and
no good."

I think that sums up the way most of the world sees
toupees.

Remember that episode of *Seinfeld* when George
came strutting in wearing a bad toupee. Elaine, in a moment of unvarnished emotion, grabbed it off his head and
tossed it out the window.

I applauded. And the world applauded with me.

Chapter 10

Figaro, Figaro, Figaro

Almost every history of haircutting has this story:

"It is recorded that the first barbers were brought from Sicily to Rome in the year of 303 B.C. In the course of a few years they had so multiplied that the city was full of them."

That particular one comes from *The Textbook of Practical and Scientific Barbering,* published in 1947 by the Educational Department of the Journeymen Barbers, Hairdressers and Cosmetologists International Union of America. Other books date the arrival a bit earlier but almost all consider that early migration as ground zero for the development of the barbershop.

Were the Sicilian barbers who paddled across the Strait of Messina to the Italian mainland the first barbers? Of course not. Barbering, like pizza, was not invented by the Italians; they just made it their own.

Once upon a time when you thought about a barber, you thought about an Italian. Figaro, the barber of Seville, was Italian. So was Perry Como. All the famous barbers were Italian.

It's not the cliché it once was—Italian barber. But

there are still plenty of Italian barbers, especially in the northeast. To find my Italian barbers, I headed to their homeland.

It's a weekday afternoon at the Three Barbers shop in Trumbull, Connecticut. All three chairs are filled and the clippers are singing. So, too, are the barbers, Nick, Tony, and Martino. Especially Martino.

Nick Clericuzio runs the shop and he introduces the visitor to the help: "This is my brother Tony. And this is Martino."

Is Martino your brother? the visitor asks.

"No, he's my grandfather."

Martino lets loose with a whoop and mock-stomps around his chair. "His grandfather? Ha, I'm his nephew."

And so it goes at Three Barbers, where the three barbers put on a full-time floor show.

"Martino, he sings," boasts Nick. "He was singing just this morning. Everybody left."

Three Barbers is an Italian barbershop to its roots.

"Mickey Sciartino started this place in 1938," says Nick. "You want to meet him? He's in the house." Nick leads the visitor out the back door, up the path, and into the attached residence to meet Michael "Mickey" Sciartino, age ninety-two.

"I was born right here in Trumbull," says Mickey. "My father was a barber in downtown Bridgeport for many years. And my grandfather before him. Back then it was all farmers lived around her."

As a boy Mickey delivered manure to farmers every morning from 5 to 8 A.M., then went to the barbershop and cut hair.

"I started out working in an eighteen-chair shop. We rented two chairs to the state of Connecticut just for learning." Those two years were a sort of on-the-job barber college.

After four years practicing his trade, he left the downtown shop and moved his barber chair to his home in Trumbull. "Everybody knew I was a barber and came to my house." Soon afterward he built an addition to the house, which still serves as a barbershop.

Shortly after Nick's family moved to this country in 1958, Mickey hired Nick to work for him.

"I was born in a barbershop," says Nick, echoing the background of many Italian barbers. "My father learned barbering in this country. He lived here till he was eleven, then he went back to Italy. At age thirteen he opened a shop. He told everybody he was thirteen and a half!

"At age nine I started lathering people. We had 250 people on contract." Those customers paid so much a month for regular shaves and haircuts. "One day a guy came in with two weeks' growth. This guy paid for two shaves and one haircut a month. One of the other barbers gave me the opportunity to shave him. I didn't finish the shave. My older brother came over and saw I was in trouble. He finished. My brother finished the chin. My father was watching. He turned me around and gave me a kick in the ass. He said, 'Next shave, you finish.'"

Nick learned his lesson. "At age eleven I gave haircuts to kids. At age thirteen I gave full haircuts. We were open 7 A.M. to 8:30 P.M. We used to do two hundred and fifty shaves a day, like an assembly line. A kid learning the trade puts soap on, then he moves up to doing the ears, then they let you shave the neck. The master barber would come over and finish the masterpiece."

His brother Tony took a different route to barbering. "Tony never worked in a barbershop in Italy," says Nick. "He was a terrific actor. He would stand in front of the shop and cry, 'I work all week long and they not pay me.' My uncle would come out and yell, 'He didn't work an hour.'"

Martino Parrella completed the Three Barbers trio when he came over in 1967. "Martino had started barbering in Rome. He had an uncle who started him at thirteen. He came over here when he was thirty-four. He's like my brother. He's the one who makes the barbershop. It's like a show. I say things. He gets upset. He gets red. He sings opera."

The clientele had changed over the years as the Trumbull area has changed. "We used to do a lot of farmers," says Nick. "We say, 'Next gentleman.' This farmer jump up and say, 'I thought I was next!'"

Nick took over the shop in 1990 when Mickey, at age eighty-three, gave it up after hip surgery. "I might be the manager or the boss but at the end of the week they make more money. They tip the help but not the boss."

A new customer enters and Nick, Tony, and Martino go back to their Three Stooges act. As Martino serenades the waiting customer, Nick tells the man, "Martino sings in church. He takes four lessons a week. He sings for baseball games. He learned the national anthem. He sings it with an accent. He sang for a Fairfield University basketball game. After he sang, the coach got fired. We blame Martino."

Deep in an office tower away from sunlight, in a shop that could be anywhere, Pino Gelsomini is plying his trade.

Pino the barber is serenading his customer, Vincenzo the chef, and Vincenzo, in turn, is serenading back.

I could transcribe the exchange, but chances are the only part you could understand would be "Volare!" That's all I could understand. But I could tell that here were two fellows who were enjoying themselves to the max.

I could give you ten tries and you would never guess where this exchange is taking place. Not in Trumbull, Connecticut. Not in New York City. Not in Chicago. It is in downtown Louisville, Kentucky, not exactly the heartbeat of Italian America.

Pino's is a recent addition to the roster of Italian barber shops in America. I had trekked all over the northeast searching for the perfect Italian shop for this book and I could have found it in my own backyard.

Because even though Pino is located in Louisville he

runs his barbershop as if it were in Italy. Oh, he speaks English to his customers, but for him Perfection Hairstyling by Pino *is* an Italian barbershop. And today he happens to be styling the hair of another in the local Italian community.

"In Italy the barbershop is entertainment," says Pino. "You find guitars, mandolins. You tell jokes, tell what you did with a girl. You become a good friend of the barber. Before you die, when making a will, maybe the barber likes fishing; you will him a fishing pole: 'This is for the barber.' Old-timers used to bring delicacies to the barber. You grow fruits; the first cherries go to the barber. Maybe you would put together a dozen of the first cherries for him."

Vincenzo agrees. "Those cherries are called *primitzia* and in the open market they would be worth a lot of money."

Vincenzo Gabrielle is the chef-owner of Louisville's finest restaurant, Vincenzo's, a five-star eatery. "The restaurant business, it's a hard business. The barbershop is the only place I can go in and relax. I go to the dentist, it's punishment. The doctor, I worry about what he's going to say. I come here and relax. I fall asleep."

Pino sighs. "It is too bad. If it continues like this it is going to disappear. I hope not The barbershop is central to the city. Now nobody wants to be a barber. They want to be a CPA."

Vincenzo sighs, too. "Look back. The barber wanted his sons to get educated. He would sacrifice so his sons would have a different life. We always want more for our kids."

Pino remembers his start in barbering. "I got to New York City, the capital of the world. I start out sweeping the floor, brushing the customer."

Vincenzo nods. "It was to keep boys occupied. Today kids have too much time on their hands."

"The barber was a city business: shoeman, barber, fishman," says Pino. "To get more well known we would make a soccer tournament. Barber versus shoeman. Barber versus fishman."

Vincenzo remembers, "In my hometown, Mola Di Bari, the barber was well established. [If you have] no money, give him two bottles of olive oil. The barber was somebody. They called him maestro."

In the Italian community the barber is still the maestro and there are still plenty of barbers named Nick, Tony, and Martino. Barbering is as Italian as pizza. Why? Nick Clericuzio, the maestro at Three Barbers in Trumbull, knows. "It was for us to be barbers."

Chapter 11

Joe's Bed-Stuy Barbershop: We Cut Heads

I visited a couple of dozen black barbershops before finding the perfect representative in Nashville.

It's a talkative sort of place—just like all barbershops—and today's discussion centers on manifest destiny. Sort of. The customer in the center chair believes that it is not manifest destiny that brought a pro football team to town, but too much emphasis on sports in society. "If they'd quit spending all that money on sports and start spending it on helping people . . ."

"But people like sports, it brings them together," counters the barber at the far chair.

There is a pause hanging in the air, along with a puff of talcum that Vernon Winfrey has just dusted onto his customer. Everyone is waiting to hear what Vernon thinks. After all this is his shop.

"People have got to help themselves," he says, in the slow, methodical manner that characterizes everything in this barbershop on the north side of Nashville, Tennessee.

Vernon Winfrey has been barbering in this spot for thirty-four years. "I rented from a man for the first ten, then I bought it."

When he started out his clientele was mostly white. "That's what the neighborhood was then." But as the neighborhood changed, so did the customers. Now it is almost all black. "There's still a few white folk come in, old customers, friends."

If the name Winfrey seems familiar, it's because you see it on TV, every afternoon, on his daughter's talk show. Vernon Winfrey's daughter is named Oprah.

When I called the Tennessee barber board looking for interesting barbershops to visit in the state, the first place the board secretary recommended was Vernon Winfrey's.

"I'm not really interested in a celebrity-dad shop," I told her.

"Oh no, you don't need to go there because of Oprah. You need to go there because of Vernon." It seems Vernon Winfrey was a name in Nashville long before his daughter anchored the noon news there. "He used to be on city council. He's done a lot of good in this community."

When you talk about black barbershops, you talk about community. Black shops are often the nerve center of the African-American communities that surround them.

Hollywood and Madison Avenue figured that out a long time ago. There's the Rogaine commercial with pro basketball player Karl Malone in the barber chair. The best scenes in Eddie Murphy's 1988 movie *Coming to America* were set in a black barbershop where two grumpy old barbers cut every customer's hair the same way. ESPN uses a black barbershop in one of its promos. Spike Lee's student film, the one that kick-started his moviemaking career, was *Joe's Bed-Stuy Barbershop: We Cut Heads*.

And in journalism when a reporter needs a quote from the black community the first stop is the barbershop.

Scratch the surface of black pop culture and you will find a barbershop. George Clinton (founder of the group Parliament Funkadelic) was a barber before he made it in the music business. He even owned a barbershop in Plainfield, New Jersey, for fifteen years. Clinton got into barbering because he was too poor to pay the five bucks for a weekly hair straightening. Soon he discovered another advantage: barbering gave him Sundays and Mondays off to work on his music.

Soul singer Keith Washington was a young barber school graduate looking to open a shop with his brother when he got his big break in music.

The grocery may have closed, the laundry may have moved out, but the black barbershop remains solidly situated in the neighborhood. It does more than survive—it thrives.

Why? In his self-published 1998 book *Barbershop Talk: The Other Side of Black Men*, Melvin Murphy argues that the black barbershop is "one of the few places where African-American men gather and do not feel threatened as black men. . . .The barbershop has provided an emotional safe-haven for men who have endured exploitation for more than two hundred years as African-American males."

Philadelphia Inquirer writer William Macklin credited it to their long tradition as pillars of the community. "Like all members of their trade, black barbers have shaped traditions, molded public opinion, arbitrated debates, built businesses as if from thin air, and garnered authority and respect often far out of proportion to their education or personal standing. But unlike many, traditional black barbers have held on, defied long hair and salon cuts, unisex trims and white flight, and maintained their positions as defenders of male fancy."

Raleigh Neal, a retired World Bank official, told the *Washington Post* the black barbershop is "one of the few things that survived integration. Why did it survive integration? Our desire to have our own groomers. You ever hear of a Chinese barbershop or a German barbershop? No. But everyone knows of the black barbershop."

But there's another reason for the flourishing of the black barbershop: the kind of talk that is the currency.

The kind of conversation I heard in Vernon Winfrey's and in other black barbershops is not the same talk I heard in other barbershops. Nowhere else do the customers debate the existence of the local pro football team, pondering whether the new stadium money could have been better spent on something else. At "white" shops they debate the trade that brought in the hotshot new quarterback or the announcement that prices for end zone tickets are rising.

Black barbershops debate these issues, too. But they go beyond, just a bit. There is a frankness and an openness in the black barbershop that is found nowhere else.

The barbershop was where former Detroit mayor Coleman Young learned about politics. In his autobiography, *Hard Stuff*, he says the debates he listened to in his neighborhood barbershop shaped his views and honed his political rhetoric. He claimed he adapted his speaking style from the authoritative tone his barber used.

Raleigh Neal heard those same kinds of conversations. "As a kid, I remember listening to the arguments, the egos. Why did the barbershop create that environment, an arrangement in which you can argue aggressively and not come to blows? And the guy on the side listening is like a judge, saying, 'He made a good argument. He didn't.' That's a dynamic."

In his 1967 book *Harlem U.S.A.*, African-American cartoonist Oliver W. Harrington described similar discussions at Harlem's Elite Barber Shop in the thirties. "Each Saturday morning some of America's top second-class citizens filled the Elite air with spirited public debate on such varied subjects as women, horses, politics, show business, surgery (both amateur and professional) and on what the s.o.b.'s were doing to keep the colored man down."

It all comes down to Murphy's law (that's Melvin Murphy in *Barbershop Talk: The Other Side of Black Men*): The black barbershop thrives because it is one of the few gathering places where African-American men can feel entirely comfortable.

The black barbershop has also been a safe house in other ways. George Clinton describes black barbershops as havens from the gang wars of the neighborhood. He recalled when he was barbering in New Jersey, "The barbershop was off-limit. People who normally didn't have any business hanging out in our neighborhood could still come to get their hair done and nobody would bother them—as long as they left when they were finished. The gangs would never get them at the barber shop or on their way out."

I was in Vernon's shop a good hour before there was even any mention of Oprah. It's not that Vernon avoids the topic of his daughter. He's proud, very proud, of her. "This place put Oprah through college," he notes. "People come in and say, 'Oprah's daddy ought to have a nicer place than this.'"

Winfrey's Barber Shop is a comfortable place, not rundown, not dirty, but comfortable. A place where you could spend the afternoon. But not luxurious. "I guess I should fix it up a bit but I don't have much time left. Besides, they say if you clean up, the rats will leave. Then I might not have any customers left."

Vernon's place is well lit with accent lighting around the ceiling. The accent lights are hidden in what looks for all the world like guttering. Vernon says, "When people ask me why I've got gutter in the shop, I tell them in case the roof leaks, it'll catch the water."

A yellowed newspaper on the back mirror, *Hillbilly Times*, a Gatlinburg souvenir paper, proclaims, "Vernon

Winfrey Named Tennessee's Best Barber." There are also
a couple of small family snapshots with Oprah in them,
but you have to go up to the mirror to tell. Mostly there
are political posters. although Vernon denies he is now or
ever has been a politician. He admits he was a member of
Nashville City Council. "I was in the political arena. But I
was never a politician."

Twelve-year-old David is Vernon's protégé. When Vernon finishes with a haircut, David hops up and brushes
the customer off. It's a courtly gesture, but this is a
courtly barbershop. In between brushings David pores
over a car stereo catalog. He's already car shopping. This
morning he found one in the paper for two hundred dollars. A customer warns him that if he buys one that cheap
it'll take him the four years until he gets his license just to
fix it up.

Vernon Winfrey was born in Mississippi, in a little
town outside Starkville. He moved to Nashville after he
got out of the service. "I always cut hair, from the age of
twelve or thirteen; people would give me ten or fifteen
cents." After the service he took a job as a janitor at Vanderbilt University. "I tell people I was the best janitor at
Vanderbilt. They say, 'janitor?' I say that job got me to the
next job."

He was saving up to go to barber college in Memphis,
"the only barber college we had in Nashville was white.
See that was before integration." When the man who
owned the Nashville barber college decided to open a little shop to train blacks, Vernon enrolled. "I didn't have to

go to learn to cut hair. I already knew how to cut hair. But I had to get my license."

Even after he got his license he continued working at a uniform company. "I was making forty-eight dollars a week. One night I cut hair and made fifteen dollars. That was cutting from four to seven. That Saturday I cut hair again and made thirty dollars. That's when I figured out I could do better cutting hair full time."

And that's what Vernon Winfrey has been doing ever since.

After clipping my ear hair and spraying me with some of the sweetest tonics my scalp has ever known, Vernon pulls the hair cloth off with a flourish. David races up to brush me off and hand me my coat.

As I leave, I can't help but admire the way I smell, the amalgam of the shaving cream, the oils, and the powders. When I meet my old college roommate Dan Pomeroy for lunch a half hour later, I do something I never did when we roomed together: I ask him to smell me.

He declines.

Chapter 12

A Captive Audience:
Barber Jokes

In his book *Parallel Lives*, the Greek biographer Plutarch records that in 4 B.C. Herod Archelaus, a well-known politician and the tetrarch of Judea, sat down in the chair of his local barbershop. "How would you like your hair trimmed?" asked the chattering barber. Archelaus responded, "In silence."

Now I have come to Canal Winchester, Ohio, 2,003 years later to meet Ed Jeffers, longtime head of the Ohio barber board. If the barbershop had an ambassador, a Mr. Barbershop, it would be Ed Jeffers. After introductions, he says he has a joke for me: "Barber: 'How do you want your hair cut?' Customer: 'In silence.'"

This could well be the oldest joke in captivity, older than "Take my wife, please."

Old and entirely representative of the way barbers practice their profession. Talk flows freely and so do the jokes.

In his Highland Park, Tennessee, shop Claude Russell charges $6.50 for a haircut. But on the mirror he has taped a sign: SILENT HAIRCUTS: $10. He says no one has ever taken him up on the offer.

Barbers know they have a reputation for talking too much. They'll tell you that, in the midst of a long-winded joke.

In fact, barbers are so well known for their jokes that in 1965 Roger Miller included a reference to the habit in his hit record "Kansas City Star":

I got credit down at the grocery store
And my barber tells me jokes.

But who would want to go into a quiet barbershop?
Conversation is what makes a barbershop.

At Vernon Winfrey's shop in North Nashville, politics is the topic of the day.

At Alpha IV barbershop in Louisville, Kentucky, sports is the topic every day, and not just because many of the athletes from the nearby University of Louisville are customers. The barbers, Big Al Roberts and Mike Sheckles, are big sports fans.

At Three Barbers in Stamford, Connecticut, they don't just talk, they sing, usually led by Martino.

In *The Art and Science of Barbering* Sherman Trusty advises barbers to "put the customer at ease as quickly as possible. . . . One right word spoken to the adult often suffices, even if it is about the trite old subject, the weather."

I haven't found a barber who doesn't follow that advice, except that one right word never seems to be enough.

Trusty goes on about the art of conversation at great length, and I do mean at great length, some six pages.

"[Conversation] is like condiments—it is very necessary, but it is easy to say too much or not enough."

He warns about being argumentative but notes that a barber can't spend all day nodding his approval. Then the customer would think him a sap.

But he does list ten topics that barbers should avoid in conversation:

"It might be better advice to say do not express yourself at all on these subjects:

1. Religion
2. Politics—who should be elected, etc.
3. The barber trade
4. Home troubles
5. Love experiences
6. Poor workmanship of other tradesmen
7. Personal problems
8. Ill manners of patrons
9. Uncomplimentary rumors
10. Financial income (his own)

That was Trusty's advice in 1958 but I don't think barbers much follow it anymore.

Another Trusty bit of advice that barbers ignore: "Continuous conversation not recommended: There should be restful elapses in conversation. Much depends on the customer; some customers like to chat and others prefer no conversation. There is the sin of commission and omission in conversation. It is easy to say too much or too little."

Trusty even offers a list of questions to ask the guy in the chair:

1. How is business?
2. Are you a native of this state? If not, ask which state.
3. How long have you lived in _____?
4. Are you working hard these days?
5. Do you think business is improving?
6. Did you read about the big fish that was caught yesterday?
7. What make of car do you have?
8. Do you enjoy the movies?
9. Do you know that Senator _____ is in town?
10. Did you know that Mr. _____ was married the other day?
11. Have you heard about Mr. _____ dying?
12. Who do you think is going to be elected governor? (But do not add your opinion.)
13. Have you ever heard Dr. _____ speak?
14. Who do you think is going to win the national heavyweight championship?
15. Do you like the East?
16. When do you think it is going to rain?
17. Do you enjoy this kind of weather?
18. How is your family?

Trusty advises that conversation should be pleasant and optimistic.

"(Bring up) non-thought-provoking subjects or questions. That is, do not bring up something that may cause the patron to have to think deeply. Only the rare individual cares to have his mind put to deep thinking."

That means if you hear someone referred to as a barbershop philosopher, the emphasis is on *barbershop*.

Claude Russell begins his banter as soon as a customer enters the shop.

"If I can't make you look better, you're ugly."

But that doesn't mean you are in for an hour of insults. Russell can turn the scorn in his own direction. "When I was born my mother said to the doctor, she said, tell me what it is so I'll know what to feed it."

And later, "I quit drinking in 1970. Pabst had to lay off half their force."

It's a floor show.

The Cubs game is on TV and when shaggy-haired reliever Rod Beck heads in from the bullpen, Russell rushes over to the set. "Change that channel. Get it off that long hair."

You won't hear your last Claude Russell joke until you walk out the door. "If you can't come back in two weeks," he warns, "send me a check."

In fact you may not hear the last one till even later, till you pass on. "I never charge for your last haircut. If you die within two weeks of a trim, I'll go to the funeral home and slip a refund check in the casket."

I have traveled to the convention of the National Association of Barber Boards of America in Las Vegas. It is the largest gathering of barbers in the world—almost a hundred are here. Ed Jeffers of Ohio and Lee Roy Tucker of Oklahoma have arrived early for the day's session. They are pouring up coffee, serving up sweet rolls, and dishing out barber jokes.

It was almost like a duel and I was right in the middle.

ED JEFFERS: "The only fight I've ever seen in a barbershop. Customer said, 'Don't put tonic on my hair. My wife will think I've been in a whorehouse.' The other customer said, 'Give me the tonic. My wife's never been in a whorehouse.'"

LEE ROY: "Barber asks the fellow, 'How do you want your hair?' He says, 'I want it sticking out on one side, cut close on the other. I want one sideburn up to here and the other one down here. I want the top chopped off and the back cut crooked.' Barber says, 'I can't cut it like that.' Customer says, 'Why not, you did last time?'"

Jimmy Hart from Louisiana wanders in and joins the fun: "Fellow came in my shop, said, 'Just give me a haircut today. I don't have time to listen to a shampoo.'"

One of the hotel servers wanders into the line of fire. Ed to hotel lady: "We're all barbers and our slogan is, 'You grow it, we mow it.'"

Charles Kirkpatrick, owner of the Cutting Edge barbershop in Little Rock, Arkansas, wanders up to join the fun. After telling me he's been in barbering so long he's gone "from Aquanet to the Internet," he contributes a

joke. "Customer comes in and says to Joe the barber,
'When would be a good time to bring my two-year-old in
to get a haircut?' Joe says, 'When he's four.'"

Barber jokes are a natural part of the culture, derived
from men spending an hour or so together in a confined
space. In the early part of the century joke books often
had entire sections of "barber jokes." The book *10,000
Jokes, Stories and Toasts for All Occasions*, published in
1940, devoted four pages to barber jokes:

*"Your hair wants cutting badly, sir," said a barber in-
sinuatingly to a customer.*
*"No, it doesn't," replied the man in the chair; "it wants
cutting nicely. You cut it badly last time."*

"Talk about torture . . ."
"Yes?"
*" . . . Nothing worse than sitting in a barber's chair
with your mouth full of lather watching the boy trying to
give another customer your new Panama hat."*

The tradition of the wisecracking barber goes back a
ways. Wehman Bros. Publishing of New York put out an
entire book called *Barber-Shop Jokes* in the twenties. It
was a minibook, to be sure, only fifty-eight pages, but
there are more than 150 jokes about barbers. Inside the
tiny covers (the book is about the size of a computer disk)
of my copy are cracks like this:

Barber (after the shave): Hair dyed, sir?
Customer (bald-headed): Yes, it died about ten years
ago.

The book continues with some of the worst barber-shop jokes you've ever heard. Fortunately I'd already heard most of them from barbers.

Chapter 13

Haircutting in Four-Part Harmony

Everybody knows about barbershop quartets and "Sweet Adeline." But how often do you really hear music in a barbershop? I got wind of such and headed to the Land of Lincoln—not Illinois, the state with the Land of Lincoln license plates, but Hodgenville, Kentucky, birthplace of Abraham Lincoln.

There are four of them so we could call them a barbershop quartet: barber Jackie Jones, in his green barber smock, strumming on the guitar accompanied by friends, one picking away on the banjo, another sawing on the fiddle, and a third thumbing the rhythm guitar.

There are no customers in Jackie Jones's Hodgenville barbershop this Saturday afternoon, just a few of Jones's chums who've dropped by for a little musical jam session. Today the music of choice is what Jones calls "southern gospel," a tight-harmony style that relies on one player knowing exactly what notes another one will be hitting.

"Sometimes we play country, sometimes bluegrass. We never know," says Jones.

They never know when the jamming mood will strike

either. So a visitor can't plan a trip to catch this barber-shop quartet, which on some days is a trio and on others a quintet or sextet.

If you didn't bring your instrument, Jackie will fish one out for you. There's a couple of acoustic guitars hanging on the wall, a fiddle dangling from the sink, an electric guitar slid under the front bench, and a steel guitar pushed up against the wall. Need a banjo? There's a couple of those in the back.

And don't worry if you break a string. Jackie has a few of those, too, on a shelf above the sink, near the Lucky Tiger hair tonic.

"They tried to get me to license this place as a music store. But I already pay $55.50 in tax. So this stays a bar-bershop . . . that happens to have a few musical supplies."

Jackie Jones, a small rotund fellow with an infectious laugh, has been barbering about as long as he's been play-ing music. He started cutting hair in 1962, shortly after winning the state Future Farmers of America contest in the novelty music category. (He picked on the guitar while blowing on a harmonica.)

As long as he's been barbering "a guitar has always been near," he says.

His shop wasn't quite so musical when he lived up in Louisville. But after a divorce in the early seventies, he moved back home to Larue County, birthplace of Abra-ham Lincoln, back home to his old jamming buddies.

"We all went to high school together. We've been play-ing together for a hundred years."

So when the music winds down—oops, here comes a customer—the radio cranks up to Jones's favorite station, playing, what else, southern gospel.

Jones's barbershop is always jumping with some kind of music.

I found one barbershop where the music is as regular as an Opry gig.

Dale Mitchell is thumbing away on his mandolin, nodding his head with the beat when he tilts backward and hits a shelf. Turning around, he's face-to-face with a bottle of Osage Rub aftershave lotion. Such are the hazards of picking and grinning in a barbershop, but Dale does it anyway—every Thursday morning at 1003 State Street in Bristol, Virginia, just a couple of blocks down the road from where country music started, or the recorded version of it anyway, with the Carter Family and Jimmie Rodgers back in the twenties.

It's the weekly bluegrass picking at Star Barbershop and on this particular morning, barber and music master Gene Boyd is busy cutting away on a customer's hair, keeping time with the music on his clippers.

It's been this way at Star Barbershop for half a century, since Gene first started cutting hair at the shop in 1950. (He bought the place in 1961.)

This morning's session starts out as a foursome: Gene on fiddle, Dale on mandolin, Jack Lewis on banjo, and Mike Breswell on stand-up bass. Then Bill Ciphers wanders in with his guitar. Pretty soon Tommy Tabor is picking his banjo in the back barber chair—under the picture of the shop's patron saint, Bill Monroe—and Ray Hutchins happens by and picks up an old guitar Gene keeps on the back sink. Then it's a full-scale picking session. Until a fellow comes by who wants his hair cut. Shucks.

Gene goes to work but the picking session never misses a beat.

It soars up for a while, then dwindles back for a time. There's a tuning break when the conversation turns to last night's Bristol City Council meeting—"I heard on radio they voted 3-1 to require them street vendors that sell pizza and Co-colas to buy a license"—then it's back to picking some more.

Gene says the picking sessions really got going back in the late fifties. "Our front here, this used to be Highway 11 W and the folks from the Grand Ole Opry, when they were on the road, would stop next door at the State Line Restaurant to eat. I had the only shower in the neighborhood so some of them would come over and pretty soon we were all picking away."

Over the years it's been a who's-who playing with a who's-that. "Weeb Pierce's been in here. Porter Wagoner. Ray there used to play with the Willis Brothers."

At 10:40 Gene finishes with his third haircut of the morning and hustles back to the band. "Let me through here to get my fiddle." He eases his way in between the banjo player and the steel guitar man. Every instrument is silent until Gene kicks it off. And suddenly an aimless bunch of players turns into a kicking band. The whole shop seems to pick up with the music. When Gene leans forward and signals the end of the tune, a fellow up front hollers out, "What was that, Gene?"

"'Boatin' Up Sandy.' That was 'Boatin' Up Sandy.'"

"That was nice."

Onie Parker steals away with his fiddle about 11 A.M. Slowly a few others wander out. But the music keeps going till Gene is ready to stop. "It's like I told that fellow—playing music is like eating pie: you just can't quit it till it's gone."

It's gone for today but next Thursday morning when Gene unbolts the door there'll be fellows waiting with banjo cases and fiddle bows.

Barbershops and music were connected long before the phrase "barbershop quartet" appeared in the lexicon.

In the seventeenth century noted memoirist Samuel Pepys recorded in his diary, "After supper my Lord called for the lieutenant's cittern, and with two candlesticks with money in them for symballs, we made barber's music, with which m'lord was well pleased."

It was the custom for barbers of the Elizabethan era to leave a flat-backed lute (Pepys called it a cittern; it was also called a gittern or an English guitar) lying around for customers to play while they waited. So originally barber's music was a lute being strummed by a shaggy man singing out of tune.

We've been singing about barbershops and in barber-shops for as long as there have been barbershops. Thrift shop troubadour Tom Waits captured the sights, sounds, and smells of the place in his 1977 paean "Barber Shop." Two decades later Rapper Yz captured his culture in a rap song of the same name. The country rockers Brother Boys recalled the heyday of the fanciest barbershop in Johnson City, Tennessee, the Majestic Hotel's tonsorial emporium, in their salute to the shop's shoeshine man, "Pop That Rag Majestic."

Every style of music has paid tribute to the barbershop or been played in the barbershop. Or both.

Which brings us to that form of music with barbershop in its name. The music now called "barbershop quartet" is an entirely American invention. But barbershop quartets are to barbershops as army music is to music—there's really not much relation. In the thousand or so barber-shop visits I have made in my lifetime (including an accelerated schedule for this book) I have never ever seen a barbershop quartet in a barbershop. I have never heard any harmonic singing. The closest I have come, outside of a place like Jackie Jones's, is the singing that typically goes on in Italian barbershops plus the occasional off-key humming of a lonely barber.

Still, the barbershop quartet is one of the ideas most closely identified with the barbershop. The name barber-shop quartet had been coined in the thirties—in America, of course—to describe a popular musical style of the day. The barbershop quartet was an outgrowth of vaude-ville shows and music hall singing. What set this new style of barbershop singing apart from other harmonizing was that the melody was sung by the second tenor, a departure from standard four-part harmonizing where the melody is sung by the highest voice, the first tenor.

Quartets had been singing in barbershops earlier than that. Author James Weldon Johnson found that black quartets were "cracking a chord" in barbershops as early as the 1870s. He identified two black southern quartets as early variants on the barbershop quartet: The American Four and The Hamtown Students. Johnson writes that in those days "every barbershop seemed to have its own quartet." He says these groups were common at places like Joe Sarpy's Cut Rate Shaving Parlor in Saint Louis.

But it wasn't until 1910 that the word "barbershop" was used in a written reference to harmonizing; it came with the publication of the song "Play That Barbershop Chord." Another early song with barbershop in the title was "Barbershop Rag," a country blues instrumental recorded by Virginia blues guitarist—and barber!—Bill Moore in 1928.

The term "barbershop quartet" was popularized in 1938 when two Tulsans, Owen Cash and Rupert Hall, founded the Society for the Preservation and Encouragement of Barbershop Quartet Singing in America, a group that is still around and now boasts 34,000 members.

When Cash and Hall met at a convention at Kansas City's Muehlebach Hotel, they discovered a mutual love of the tight vocal harmonies of the barbershop quartet and decided to do something about it. Their group began as a lark: calling themselves "Rupert Hall, Royal Keeper of the Minor Keys, and O. C. Cash, Third Temporary Assistant

Vice Chairman," they staged a songfest when they got back home on the roof garden of the Tulsa Club on April 11, 1938. Only twenty-six people attended that first gathering but by the third singing congress the group had grown to 150. The music that flowed from the rooftop actually caused a traffic jam outside the hotel. Police were called, a reporter followed, and next thing Cash knew he was bluffing his way through a newspaper interview, calling his club a national organization and boasting of branches in Saint Louis and Kansas City, failing to mention these branches were actually just groups of friends. Associated Press and United Press International picked up the story and soon there really were SPEBSQSA branches in Saint Louis, Kansas City, and all over. Today there are almost as many members of the Society for the Preservation and Encouragement of Barbershop Quartet Singing in America as there are barbershops.

A customer entered Jackie Jones's barbershop during the jam session so Jones excused himself from picking to do a little cutting. But you can tell he's antsy to get playing again. He finishes and removes the hair cloth from the fellow's front but the customer doesn't move out of the chair. "Go on and play some more of that music," he says.

Jones is happy to oblige. Soon the floor is shaking, Charlie is picking away on his banjo and Jones is warbling praise to the Lord. And cars passing on the street out front give a short honk in salute.

Chapter 14

Famous Barbers I Have Known

There's a picture of *The Andy Griffith Show's* Floyd the Barber on the wall at Floyd's City Barbershop in Mount Airy, North Carolina. In fact there's a picture of Floyd on the wall in about half of America's barbershops. But ask about Floyd at Floyd's Barbershop in Winfield, West Virginia, and co-owner Jim Daley points to a mounted boar's head on the wall. "That's Floyd," he grins. And everyone in the shop laughs.

Everybody knows who Floyd is—he's the prissy barber portrayed memorably for almost a decade by actor Howard McNear.

Four decades after it first debuted, *The Andy Griffith Show* is still going strong, rerun daily on cable channels.

People love Andy and Barney, Aunt Bee and little Opie, Gomer and Goober. And they love Floyd the Barber.

Floyd Lawson was the gentlest character on *The Andy Griffith Show,* which is saying a lot considering the overall gentility of Mayberry's residents. Oh, he could get riled up. After all, he did poke Charlie Foley in the nose back in 1946 during an argument over a shave. But Floyd portrayed the characteristics that have made barbers what they are for centuries. Sherman Trusty had outlined them a few years earlier in his trusty barber's manual: "The barber should be alert to the fact that it is not entirely what he does nor how well he discharges his skill, but how he does it that influences customers and makes them continue to patronize his shop."

Trusty dispensed considerable advice about interacting with the customer but Floyd paid closest attention to three tenets:

Consistently wear a cheerful countenance.
Have a ready smile.
Maintain a good posture.

That made Floyd's Barbershop what Aunt Bee called "the center of the town's activities for years."

Opie had a different take on the place. "Say, Pa, when I get older can I loaf around the barbershop, too?"

Andy's response was a bit defensive. "Well, I wouldn't call it loafing, Opie."

"Gee, Pa. You don't do anything there. You just sit around and play checkers and talk and grunt."

One exchange on the show reminded me of the banter at my barber Wib's. When Barney exclaimed, "Next time I want a haircut, I'm gonna stick my head in a pencil sharpener," Floyd calmly replied, "Sure, and it'll fit, too."

The barber has made many famous entrances on stage, screen, and television over the years.

In today's world Mayberry's Floyd is probably the most famous barber. But it wasn't that long ago that Figaro was the most famous fictional barber.

Figaro was the title character in *The Barber of Seville,* a play written by French watchmaker Pierre-Augustin Caron de Beaumarchais in 1775, turned into an opera by Gioacchino Rossini in 1816, and popularized by Alfalfa in the *Little Rascals* in the thirties.

Figaro was a matchmaker of sorts, trying to hook up the beautiful Rosina with her young suitor Count Almaviva while foiling Dr. Bartolo, her ward, an old guy who wanted to marry her.

At the other end of the barber pole is the celebrated Sweeney Todd, Demon barber of Fleet Street, the homicidal hairstylist of the Stephen Sondheim musical. A visit to Todd's barbershop in Old London of the nineteenth century spelled death for unsuspecting customers who wanted only a shave but got a slit throat instead. "Down you go!" Todd would cry as the barber's chair dropped into the floor, sending the victim plummeting to the cellar below, where dear Mrs. Lovett would bake the clean-shaven into meat pies.

Film has given us some pretty memorable barbers, too. In his book *The 247 Best Movie Scenes in Film History,* Sanford Levine compiled a list of the best haircut scenes in movies.

He calls the haircut Humphrey Bogart receives in *The*

Treasure of the Sierra Madre "one of the three worst hair-cuts in Western film history. Yet, when the barber shows Bogart how it looks in the back, he meekly nods, okay. Why?" Levine thinks maybe Bogart didn't want to hurt the barber's feelings.

He likes the haircut scene in *Yellowbeard* even though he says the screenwriters telegraph their punch. "Yellow-beard's son has committed a treasure map to memory and tattooed it to the top of his head in case he forgets where the treasure map is. . . . When Yellowbeard's son shows a lapse of memory at the wrong moment, Yellowbeard (Graham Chapman) takes out his saber and gives his son what may be the fastest and funniest haircut in screen history."

He found the best haircut line in Woody Allen's *Hannah and Her Sisters.* Maureen O'Sullivan refers to her husband Lloyd Nolan as "This haircut that passes for a man."

The most unbelievable haircut scene, according to Levine, comes from *Jailhouse Rock* (1957). "A woman at a bar says to Presley, 'You got nice hair.' Before we know it, Presley is in his cell waiting to get a haircut. . . . The tension heightens markedly when his cellmate, Mickey Shaughnessy, tells Presley that prison barbers being what they are, it will cost him three packs of cigarettes to get a good haircut."

But when the prison barber arrives he snips just three seconds, barely taking any off the sides.

In real life the most famous "barber" of the fifties wasn't a barber at all. Sal "The Barber" Maglie, was a hard-throwing pitcher for the Giants and Dodgers with a ferocious fastball. I'm sure if they'd had radar guns in the forties he would have clocked in the nineties. He was also fearless and if a batter tried to dig in on Sal he could expect a little chin music—a high hard one at the chin, a brush-off pitch to get him back from the plate, "shaving" him with the horsehide. That's where his nickname "The Barber" came from.

Sal the Barber wasn't a barber. But Perry Como the singer was a barber. So was actor Joe Pesci. In fact Pesci was a failed actor who had gone back to barbering when Martin Scorsese and Bobby De Niro were scouting locations for *Raging Bull*. They went in his shop, loved the little guy, and brought him back to acting.

George Clinton, the godfather of funk, was a barber. So was soul singer Keith Washington. Rosa Parks, whose refusal to move to the back of a Birmingham, Alabama, bus sparked the Civil Rights movement, was married to a barber.

And then there's Floyd, all the real Floyds across the country. Famous by an accident of birth name.

Afterword:
Too Many Haircuts

Police officer Mike Day gave me that big grin of his. "What's different about you? I didn't even recognize you when I walked in." Officer Day patrols my neighborhood and I've known him for ten years.

What's different about me? "Too many haircuts," I told him.

I'd been getting a haircut every week—sometimes even more often than that—for a year. At one of my last haircuts, the Acapulco Plaza Barbershop in Topeka, Kansas, master barber Greg Sandate gave me the quizzical look I've been seeing for the past year from barbers accustomed to customers coming in every four to six weeks.

"How do you want me to cut it?" he asked, making it clear that I really didn't need a haircut.

"Take about half of it off," I said. And he did. Only this time about half was about half of half an inch.

You could say the barber business is a growth industry but it hasn't been growing lately.

There were some 118,000 barbershops in this country in 1939. A quarter century later, in 1963, that number had dropped to around 106,000. Then the Beatles arrived and the number of barbershops plummeted to 69,000 in 1978.

It's been a downhill roll ever since: some 51,000 barbershops in 1990; barely 45,000 in 1995, the latest year for which the government has statistics.

Whether the shaving mug is half-empty or half-full depends on your point of view. At least there are still 45,000 places where you can go to get your hair cut, your neck shaved, and your funny bone tickled.

What does the future hold for the barber?

In 1970 the folks at Coiffure Masculine Hair Institute peered in a crystal ball for the book *The History of Hair* and made this timely prediction: "By the year 2001, 75 percent of the male population will be wearing wigs." The prognosticators noted that these wigs would be fashion accessories, rather than baldness camouflage. Not exactly on the mark, but read on. "In addition it is predicted that by the year 2001 baldness will be obsolete. . . . Black and brown color sprays will be used to darken balding areas." They got that one right—just turn on late-night television and catch Ron Popeil's infomercial for GLH (Good Looking Hair). They continued, "In general hair will be longer and fuller than it is worn today. However color will be the most important aspect of men's hairstyling. . . . By the year 2001, 75 percent of the male population will resort to hair coloring of some kind." Not exactly on the money but not far off: the actual number today is closer to 20 percent. But pretty prescient.

Charles DeZembler, author of a 1939 history of hair entitled *Once Over Lightly*, also tried his hand at hair handicapping. "As for the future of the barber, I believe it is largely in his own hands. It is bright, as I view it, even if it does have its moments of recession, depression and even despondency. Today there are many barbershops in the United States. In the world at large, it's a safe guess that hair will continue to move off the head of the man and come back, to forsake his face and then, after an interval, move back. That's what it has been doing in the past."

Charles Kirkpatrick, owner of the Cutting Edge barbershop in Little Rock, Arkansas, and an officer of the National Barber Board, insists barbers are not a vanishing breed. He agrees with DeZembler—there are recessions and depressions and periods of despondency for barbers. But it's not so bad. "There are plenty of jobs for barbers. There just aren't as many people who want to fill them." The day I talked to him, he said he had three openings in the state of Arkansas that he could fill immediately, if he could find a barber.

He sort of tried to get me to consider barber college.

It's hard to get a young boy—or girl—to sign up for a life of standing on his feet with no pot of gold at the end of the rainbow. But DeZembler is right: there is always going to be a need for barbers.

Maybe a few people will read this book and think maybe it wasn't so bad getting their hair cut from a guy who told them jokes and stories about the neighborhood. Maybe stylists will go out of style and people will get back on the barbershop bandwagon.

Now when I consider slipping in a chain shop for a quick cut, I consider the advice proffered in an 1883 edition of the trade magazine *The Barber's Shop:*

Do not be deterred by any doubtful authority that tells you two years of an old man's life is wasted by attending the barber's shop. Walk in frankly and often. Accept the invitation of the pole. Think of Marc Anthony who got himself barbered ten times over before going to feast with Cleopatra, the voluptuous dark-eyed queen of Egypt. The genial atmosphere and pleasant chat of the place will not only enliven the passing hour but will lengthen out your days to such an extent that a year or two, more of less, will never be missed.

If you saw my picture on the back of this book, or if you remember my picture from any of my previous nine books, many of which are still in print and come highly recommended by the author, or if you know me in real life—hi, Mom!—then you may be asking:

Why did a bald man write a book about barbershops?

You're not the first. When I told my friend Bob Moody, he asked the same question, prefaced by "no offense." No offense taken. Actually I think his exact phrase was: What the hell is a bald man doing writing a book about barber-shops? It's a legitimate question. Why? Because when it comes down to it, hair-cutting has very little to do with why we go to a particular barbershop.

We bald men just learn that lesson earlier than you curly-headed fops.

I started going bald in college—thank you, God. I remember combing my hair in the communal bathroom when my friend Bevo sneaked up behind, gave me the evil eye, and then tossed off this remark: "You're going bald." That is not what a twenty-one-year-old wants to hear, especially a single, un-girlfriended twenty-one-year-old. I'd been thinking about it—that's why I was peering so intently at my hair in the mirror. But out of my mouth came these words: "I've always had a high forehead."

I believed that. I believed that because I wanted to believe that.

But as the years crept by I noticed my high forehead getting higher and higher. At first I denied it. My part kept getting lower and lower on the side of my head until I had one of those corrupt-politician haircuts: all wispy on top with a part just above the ear. The cover-up lasted about two years. I was single, after all and, Kojak notwithstanding, I didn't think the ladies liked the bare brow look.

At the time Gillette had just come out with a new hair-spray for men, Command, and I personally kept that product on the market for my two years of cover-up. I even carried a second can in the car.

Then one day I got tired of living in fear of the wind.

I went back home to my dear old bald barber J. Fred and told him to get rid of the comb-over.

I finally accepted being bald. And what a relief that was.

Over the past years when people have asked what I'm working on and I've told them a book about barbershops, there hasn't been a single person who didn't have a story. Just this morning Helen Carter, a colleague at the University of Louisville, told me how her husband had been enamored of his barber when he was young. "He was in an accident when he was seventeen—he got hit by a train—and he sort of took up with the local barber. He had moved to a town where he didn't know anybody and the barber sort of took him under his wing. The barber was about forty so it was a fatherly kind of thing. When our son was born, he wasn't twenty minutes out of the hospital than we had to drive to that barbershop to let that barber see him. He snipped off a lock of his hair for us."

Barbers over the years have been confidants, friends, father figures. They've supplied us with news, gossip, and corny jokes. And, oh yeah, they've cut our hair. How do you replace something like that in a culture?

Maybe some people are content to have good-looking hair and an empty soul, but for me the character of the barbershop is the most important thing about it. A good haircut has very little to do with a good barbershop.

To wind it all up, I went back to Wib's, the barbershop where this whole thing started. It was a rare morning, just Wib and me, none of the regulars.

"What's up, Wib?" I asked. I knew he'd have an answer.

"I just sit here in my old shoeshine chair in the window and watch the world go by." Business was slow, he said.

As I approached the end of this book, I'd been wondering about Wib. He's getting up toward retirement age and I was concerned I was going to have to find a new barber. He told me he signed a twenty-year lease eighteen years ago. It runs out in 2002. What happens then? I wondered aloud. "I'm sure they'll double my rent," he acknowledged. I asked because an expired lease was what put my father out of the hardware business after thirty years.

"I'm not thinking about retirement," Wib Scarboro assured me. "As long as I got my health . . ." Then he chuckled. ". . . And I don't have to work, I'm gonna keep at it."

Acknowledgments

A round of applause, please, for the following people, none of whom needs an introduction or a haircut:

Ed Jeffers, owner of the Barbershop Museum in Canal Winchester, Ohio, and a man who knows absolutely everything about barbers and barbershops. And also knows every barber joke.

A couple of guys who'll talk about anything, if you just buy them lunch, Larry Magnes and David Inman.

Helpful friends: Bob Moody, Dan Pomeroy, David Vish, Chris Wohlwend, Charlie Willard, Al Futrell, Bart Collins, Joy Hart, John Monberg, Stuart Esrock, Rod Irvin, Tom McNeer, Marsha McNeer, David Jenkins, Steve Vest, Patti George, Greg Johnson, Jena Monahan, the late great Maureen McNerney, Bob Hill.

Researcher Margaret Deegan.

Jenny at Koken barber chairs.

Joseph Randall Murphy at Hairpeople.

Alan Beecher, and Kathy at Iowa Beauty Supply.

The helpful folks at the Historical Society of the Wilmington, Delaware, Public Library.

Jeffery Stein, curator at New York Historical Services and Historic Preservation Society.

The research staff at the Louisville Free Public Library.

Everyone I left out.

And all these folks at the state barber boards around America: Arkansas, Charles Kirkpatrick; California, James Knauss; Colorado, O. B. McClinton; Connecticut, Jim Dinneen; Florida, Melissa Howard; Idaho, Marilyn London; Indiana, James Dye, Karl Konopasek, and Tracy Hicks; Iowa, Margie Jass, Roxanne Sparks, and Jerry Dickie; Iowa, Stu Preston; Kentucky, Russell Carrithers, Ken Watson, Dallas Cook, Jesse Weekly, Douglas Clapper, Anna Marie Johnson, and Glenda Neely; Louisiana, Wayne Dargle; Maine, Jerry Betts and Sonya Weedberry; Maryland, Kathleen Harryman, Phil Mazza, and John Gatton; Massachusetts, Arthur Chidlovski; Minnesota, Maureen Tibbetts, Frank Wyland, and Kenneth Kirkpatrick; Mississippi, Saundra Clark, Clinton Brock, Stanley McKee, Robert Rabin, and Jim Adams; Montana, Paulette Brandon; Nebraska, Ronald Pella, Carol Ann Gray, and Judy Hansen; New Hampshire, Linda Elliott and Theresa Pare; New Mexico, Margie Sanchez; New York, Phillip Lord, and Justin McShea; North Dakota, Marlene Sax and Jill Mrnak; Ohio, Clyde Schafer, Edwin Jeffers, and Lisa Leibfacher; Oklahoma, Kay Washington and Leroy Tucker; Oregon, Gordon Scarborough and Garner Poole; Pennsylvania, Julie Clouse, Larry and Jayne Christman; Rhode Island, Linda Acciardo and Michelle

Monroe; South Carolina, Shanda Johnson; South Dakota, Susan Monge, Jamie Damon, Charles Huber, and Ronda Gibson; Tennessee, Evelyn Griffin; Texas, Diane Lamonte; Utah, Pamela Johnson and Marty Simon; Washington, Randy Renfroe and Craig Conway; West Virginia, Larry Absten, John Roland Palmer, and Hubert B. Samples; Wisconsin, Ruby Jackson and Ryan Lepianka; Wyoming, Douglas Edgell.

And a standing ovation for:

Michael O'Brien, for the flattering photo of me.

My editor, Constance Herndon, for the necessary slices and dices.

My agent, Kris Dahl, for the groundwork.

Wib, for the haircuts.

My research assistant, Ashley Simon, for effort above and beyond. She told me she doesn't know what to do now that this project is over. "I'm so used to reading everything I can about barbershops. I was visiting a girlfriend and sitting at her computer, when I noticed I had absentmindedly typed in a search for *barbershop*."

And, of course, the fam.

About the Author

Vince Staten was born and raised in Kingsport, Tennessee. A graduate of Duke University and the University of Tennessee, his articles have appeared in *Food & Wine*, *Bon Appétit*, and *The New York Times*. He is the author of nine previous books, including *Did Monkeys Invent the Monkey Wrench?* and *Do Pharmacists Sell Farms?* (reissued as *Did Trojans Use Trojans?*). Staten, who is on the faculty of the University of Louisville, lives in Prospect, Kentucky. His current barbershop is Wib's, "Home of the Happy Haircut."